Chester says

BE YOUR OWN BOSS

Volume 2
Running and Growing a Services Business

Rodney Richards
George I. Martin, EdD

IMPORTANT NOTICES

Chester says Be Your Own Boss Volume 2
Copyright © 2024 Rodney Richards and George I. Martin

All rights reserved

No part of this book or its contents can or may be used, saved, published, transmitted, distributed, or reproduced in any form in any media by any means without permission of the author and publisher, except by a reviewer who may quote brief passages in a review. For rights and permissions send written requests to 1950ablia@gmail.com.

Print ISBN 979-8986360362
Ebook ISBN 979-8986360379

Library of Congress LCCN 2024903756

Front cover art designed and created by Jesse Richards.
Edited by Rodney Richards
Published by ABLiA Media LLC, Hamilton NJ, USA

Second edition

Disclaimers

Contents reflect experiences and opinions of the authors. Neither the authors nor the publisher are engaged in rendering legal, technical, investment, or financial services. Consult with a professional when appropriate.

While the authors and publisher have used their best efforts in preparing this book, they make no representations or warranties regarding the accuracy or completeness of its contents and specifically disclaim any implied warranties of merchantability or fitness for a particular purpose.

Quotations, facts, details, and images are derived from publicly available sources, owned or licensed by the authors, or used with permission. Links shown may have changed. References to products, brands, services, logos, or company names are neither endorsements nor disapprovals, and may be trademarked. AI was not used to create or enhance any text or images.

Examples, advice, and strategies may not be suitable for your situation.

Neither the authors nor the publisher shall be liable for any loss of profit or any other commercial damages, including but not limited to special, incidental, consequential, personal, or other damages.

Table of Contents

- To I
- **PREFACE AND SHORT INTRO** I
  - Business must have stability III
- **PART THREE: OPERATE** 1
  - CHAPTER 18 Spread the news 1
    - Become known 1
    - Catch customers 3
    - Attract attention 4
  - CHAPTER 19 Principles of service 6
    - What makes great service? 8
    - The Age of Service 9
    - What business takes 10
    - Stay neutral, but… 10
    - Help others 11
  - CHAPTER 20 Buyers and Sellers 12
    - Understand your buyer 14
    - Laws and agreements 15
    - Elements of contracts 16
    - "Contract" is not a dirty word 17
    - Service Agreements 20
  - CHAPTER 21 How to sell 20
    - Two kinds of purchases 20
    - Types of selling 22
    - Upselling 22
    - What's your buyer's budget? 23
    - Pricing 24
    - Margins 24
    - Recurring revenue 25
  - CHAPTER 22 Finances 27
    - Use professionals 27
    - Budget your business 30
    - The importance of reporting 34
    - The Ledger 35
  - CHAPTER 23 Banking 36
    - Getting paid 37
    - Use Direct Deposit or Payment 38
  - CHAPTER 24 Track your credit 39
    - Using credit 41
    - Safeguard your credit 44
    - Use cash 45
  - CHAPTER 25 Backbones of business 46
    - Invoicing 46
    - Save and issue receipts 47

  Use timely tools and resources 48
  Reinvest from profits 49
 CHAPTER 26 DEATH AND BUSINESS TAXES 50
  Income taxes 50
  Business taxes 51
  Sales tax 53
  Employee taxes 54
  Self-employment tax 55
  Credits and tax deductions 55
 CHAPTER 27 ONLY 18 HOURS IN A DAY 58
  Do the work but 59
  Prioritizing tips 60
  Broken promises 61
 CHAPTER 28 GODS OF THE 21ST CENTURY 62
  Online everything 62
  Software is king 63
  We users come last 64
  Support at your fingertips 66
  Cyberpol 68
 CHAPTER 29 SECURITY DOESN'T EXIST 69
  Run scans 69
  Passwords and security 70
  Keep your house in order 71
  Use utility programs 72
  Check your browser 73
  When your browser is corrupt 76
 CHAPTER 30 COMPUTER GOTCHAS AND FIXES 77
  Phishing attacks 77
  Save your bacon 79
  Ad blockers 82
  Unclog storage 82
 CHAPTER 31 "I'VE BEEN ROBBED!" 83
  Secure your possessions 83
 CHAPTER 32 POLITICS AND POLICIES 86
  The customer 90
  You as owner 91
  Assume nothing 92

PART FOUR GROW **94**

 CHAPTER 33 BETTER OPPORTUNITIES 94
  The move turns superior 96
  Business of the Month 97
 CHAPTER 34 DO BETTER THAN BREAKEVEN 98
  Get off the ground 101
  Refine your brand 104

CHAPTER 35 SALES AND MARKETING GOALS 105
   Set goals or fail 107
   Spending goals 108
   What are you really selling? 109
   Build your reputation 110
   Learn how to sell 111
CHAPTER 36 WHAT YOU NEED 112
   You must have a webpage 112
   Include a CTA and sales page 113
   Get reviews and do surveys 114
   Surveys 115
   The Sunk Cost Fallacy 115
   Case studies 116
CHAPTER 37 REACH YOUR MARKET 117
   Marketing versus advertising 118
   Refine your Marketing Plan 119
   The dirty laundry of retail 121
   The dirty laundry of advertising 123
   Primary concerns as an advertiser 124
   What is CTR? 125
   The best ads 126
CHAPTER 38 TARGET AND ADVERTISE 129
   Reach the globe, but… 129
   Physical advertising signs 132
   Advertising online 135
   My they've made it complex! 137
   Market Share 137
CHAPTER 39 ADVERTISING NITTY-GRITTYS 138
   Who to target 138
   Ad campaigns 139
   Amazon vs Facebook 140
   Google and other ads 142
   Ad creation tips 143
CHAPTER 40 REFINE MARKETING 144
   Marketing services and products 146
   Use AI tools 146
   Automation 148
   Brainstorming 149
   Funneling 152
   Cross-Promotion 152
   Ride the sales wave 153
CHAPTER 41 SHUTTING DOWN AND RESTARTING 154
   Changing gears 154
   A new enterprise 155
CHAPTER 42 TARGETED SALES TECHNIQUES 157

> *Reach actual needs* 158
> *You are the Sower* 161
> *Email reaches out directly* 162
> *Ecommerce automation* 164

CHAPTER 43 AVENUES OF OUTREACH 165
> *TV and Radio* 166
> *Podcasts* 168
> *Webinars* 168
> *Newspapers* 169
> *Cold calling* 171
> *Scammed* 173

CHAPTER 44 WEBSITE AND SEO 175
> *Perfect your website* 176
> *Search engines* 177
> *Make business profiles* 179
> *Cookies, cookies, cookies* 180

CHAPTER 45 SOCIAL MEDIA 181
> *How it should work* 184
> *Summary on social media* 185

CHAPTER 46 MERCHANT SERVICES 186
> *FinTech Firms* 187
> *Collecting sales taxes* 188

CHAPTER 47 EXPAND YOUR INFLUENCE 189
> *Coddle influencers* 190
> *Reach public influencers* 193
> *Time is a friend... or enemy* 194

CHAPTER 48 NETWORK AND AFFILIATE 194
> *Affiliations are good, but...* 199
> *Credentials are best* 200

CHAPTER 49 CARTING AWAY OUR MONEY 202
> *Do the math* 203

CHAPTER 50 DIRECT AND INDIRECT MARKETING 204
> *Indirect marketing* 207
> *QR Coding* 208
> *Know and serve your community* 209
> *Become known online* 210

CHAPTER 51 VENUE VENTURES 211
> *Indoor venues* 211
> *Make sales by walking around* 214
> *Offers out of the blue* 216
> *Volunteer* 217
> *Outdoor venues* 218

CHAPTER 52 REFERRALS AND AFFILIATES 220
> *Affiliate marketing and revenue* 221
> *Don't get hemmed in* 222

- Chapter 53 Branch out and In 222
  - *Expand* *225*
  - *Surveys grow your business* *230*
  - *Partnering* *232*
  - *Movie ticket anyone?* *232*
- Chapter 54 Aftershock 234
- Chapter 55 Downsizing 235
  - *Decide the income you need* *236*
  - *Whether young, in between, or old* *237*
  - *Learning Center reflections* *240*
  - *LLC reflections* *242*
- Epilogue to Volume 2 242
  - *Making business work—George & Ilene* *243*
  - *Life and joy can come together—Rod* *244*
- Appendix A Sample 246
- Appendix B Sample Rack Cards 249
- Other Resources 250

ABOUT THE AUTHORS 251

TO

Every person who has or will start a business.
   Thank you for your courage, passion, determination, and hopes and dreams.
   Without you, humanity will be bereft of the products, goods, and services that keep it well and alive.
   Without you, life is an unbearable hardship.

Janet, my inspirer, cheerleader, confidant, great love, and best friend in the worlds God has created or will create. — Rod

Ilene, your consummate skill in scheduling and in knowing every detail of our business, was and continues to be invaluable.
— George

PREFACE and SHORT INTRO

Throughout this volume, you will learn how to:
• Run a top shelf company
• Get more leads
• Get more referrals
• Get more sales

It takes guts to start a business, and you showed them.
   We are so glad you pushed ahead with your idea to start and open a small business in America. **It takes courage and sacrifice to run any kind of business well and be successful.**
   George and his wife Ilene showed with their C-Corp storefront, the Chesterfield Learning Center for tutoring, that opening for them was harder and more costly but worked.

Working from home with a PC like it is for Rod with his ABLiA Media LLC for writing, editing, and publishing, was much easier and less costly, and just as rewarding.

Whether a storefront, home business, food truck, or webpage, the key to success is following good advice and experience, staying focused, and being firm in principle, flexible in details.

It doesn't matter what your business is or its size. Tips, information, specifics, steps, and insights that follow in this Volume 2 will help you because it can be overwhelming.

It's the Information Age. That means overload too.

We wrote both volumes to make sure you learn the best.

You will find some critical points repeated in different ways throughout, however, we promise it won't be boring or trite. As businesspeople ourselves we know what it's like—difficult. But it's worth it, as 33 million U.S. small businesses know.

In any setting, it takes determination, smarts, vision, and drive to do well in this world of competition. This book will arm you so you don't fail. It will cite sources, tools, and wisdom you need to thrive and make sales.

We have every wish and desire to see you through your journey and become a well-known brand and a successful solopreneur or entrepreneur.

You are your own boss, a great one.

Show the world make you're made of.

INTRO

In *Chester says Be Your Own Boss Volume 1*, we highlighted preparations, startup, and opening a services business for a few hundred dollars or thousands. Targeted chapters laid out basics, insights, tips, and what not to do from forming a business via state registration—gaining a Formation/ Authorization Certificate and filing a tax status, through a Grand Opening.

Passion, abilities, resources, and goals cement entrepreneurial vision. No one else will make your company successful. Navigating the hills and valleys of commerce and ecommerce depends on the reputation you make for yourself.

The SBA Office of Advocacy reported that those 33.3 million small businesses in the U.S. account for 99.9% of U.S. businesses. Of these, 43.4% are owned by women, 6.1% by veterans, 14.5% by Hispanics, and 20.4% by racial minorities. Over 69% of businesses start at home.

Now you own one too. **Business, like life, is about you.**

From birth to grave every life revolves around their own needs and wants, then those of others, like putting your breathing mask on first during an emergency plane landing, then your child's, even though you love your child more than you do yourself. We must first take care of ourselves to help others.

Running a business means taking care of ourselves to help others. **A positive outlook and shared enthusiasm will catch fire.** But unlike the movie *Field of Dreams*, just because you build it doesn't mean Shoeless Joe or buyers will come. Read on, jot notes, put colored sticky tabs on pages, make smart decisions, and take action to increase your chances.

Every person wants to be loved, valued, and part of a family or tribe. If you show people respect and care, they will be your friends, fans, and customers for life. That's how to run and grow any business.

But business and life require stability and certainty to thrive.

Business must have stability

Chester says: *Tottering governments, instability, insecurity, and uncertainty kill business and life.*

You know the drill; you live the drill. It's the society/ culture you're part of. If lucky through birth or circumstance, or your own determination and will, you live in a normal, semi-peaceful town, city, state, and nation. The average person wants to live, work, start or raise a family or be with someone they love, enjoy friends, make sure everyone's okay, and eat, drink, laugh, pray, celebrate, or cry together.

Just to live in peace, have a good job, and be stable, is tough anywhere today.

Commerce, ecommerce, business, government, love, life, work, everything, needs stability to operate.

    Long-ago, three societal institutions emerged to provide stability: Government, meant to serve and protect; Business, people helping people; and Religion, the foundation of moral and spiritual truth.

    Fear, uncertainty, doubt; unfairness, selfishness, greed; oppression, crime, bad laws, division; hatred, violence, conflict, and war destroy normalcy. Innocent lives are lost that needn't be. Society and institutions or those in them must change.

    No one can exist or grow a business under FUBAR circumstances. Only when we work together, mandate justice, and hold similar values and principles, can we hope to create a global civilization. **Your business and society rely on stability and unity.** Like Wall Street, nothing upsets governments, religion, economies, markets, commerce, people, and life worse than uncertainty. It doesn't matter where, why, when, or what your product or service is, or how it's provided, instability will destroy it.

    As both business owner and operator, the best way to foster stability is to know what you need to do and do it timely, using up-to-date knowledge and advice.

    We put this book together for that purpose and one more: to show business principles which will guide you to the success you want.

    Two words will make it happen: Be human.

Rod (R) & George (G)

PART THREE: OPERATE

Chapter 18 Spread the news

C hester says: ***It's easy to get noticed. Staying noticed takes relationship-building.***

Become known

You opened your own business! That's exciting and wonderful!

You should be rightfully pleased to be your own boss. You offer a great service and want everyone to know. You can imagine success.

But everyone starts out in obscurity. Unless we had famous parents like JFK and Jackie, showed a viral TikTok video like Zack King, were lucky to get a TV spot on Kelly & Mark, or we saved a child from a fire, the mass of people won't know who we are.

You are determined to change that obscurity.

You don't need the patience of Job for your new company to become a household name with millions of clients or customers, like the 185 years it took Procter & Gamble. Look at Hula-Hoops, iPhones, Nintendo, YouTube, ChatGPT, hit songs, movies, Post-it Notes, or things or people that had overnight success and wide acceptance. Who would have guessed?

Since commercial radio broadcasts began in 1919, everything is seen or heard "online" instantly to wide audiences. TV made that broader starting 9 years later, especially in the '50s. Then came computers and smartphones. Since 2000, ecommerce now buys and sells anything online, online banking performs money transfers and pays bills, and websites and phone apps grant digital services wirelessly.

Our heads spin like dreidels from the miracles that surround us in this modern age.

How do we initially find out about anything? We are influenced by what we hear and see in our travels; other folks or friends, parents, teachers; signs or ads, on TV or radio stations;

internet searches; posts on Facebook, etc. They catch our eyeballs and ears, hearts, minds, and spark desire. If we hear or see it more than once, it has a higher chance of influencing us.

And the most effective influencers are people we know or sources we trust.

If I need a new tv or barbecue grill, I ask people I know what they use, and how well it works. If I need a plumber I call my realtor friend for a number. If a limb falls in my yard, it's my brother Chaz and his team. We trust or are willing to try out, recommendations from those we know before we check ads on the internet or call a number in an ad.

Build business longevity on reputation, trust, and relationships. Familiarity, appearances, and perceptions count. Become known by:

- Saying "Hi" verbally or digitally
- Being confident word will spread
- Offering quality products or services
- Telling relatives, friends, acquaintances, and strangers
- Appealing to emotion and intelligence
- Having a company name that resonates and is trusted
- Being consistent with logos, marketing materials, social media posts and advertising
- Answering texts and emails (but screen calls)
- Making your website dynamic not static
- Capturing potential client email addresses and names
- Making new connections and build communities
- Being professional
- Using automated marketing tools and AI
- Getting involved locally with like-minded groups
- Being passionate.

Provide a needful or desirable product or service. Highlight its benefits and outcomes.

People trust familiarity, even cling to it, before they change or embrace the new to replace the old. Make your newness seem familiar and trustworthy.

Teach unknown things in terms of what people know.

A 2nd-grader can't understand rocket science. They must learn earth science and gravity, Math, Algebra, Geometry, Trig, then Calculus, followed up with Astronomy. Concrete and physical examples and experiments dot every concept learned.
**Same goes when selling about your product or service.
Only systematic steps get you there.**

Catch customers

You fish for contacts and customers in a large pond—life. You know this pond is huge, and you don't know those in it. Some people in it are like you, most others are different.

How do you catch the most fish, or people?

Other fishers told you where to find prospects **(market data)**. You have your fishing gear, rod, reel, tackle box, and must decide the bait **(tools)**. Or you go big with a boat and nets, maybe a crew. **(refine your goals)**

Cast a line out or cast a net. **(Specific targeted pages on your website and in your ads. For one, or many?)**

Offer something. What bait are you using? What attracts fish? **(Discounts, limited offers, superior quality)**

Do you know what type of fish you are trying to catch? There are so many. **(User/customer profiles)**

Are you at the place where you know the fish are? **(Targeted audience/ targeted platform)**

If you cast your rod, are you prepared to wait? Or if using a net, are you prepared to haul the load up onto your boat? **(Can you handle the response?)**

Some will get away. Can you find them again? **(Automated systems, capturing emails, follow-ups)**

It's not a perfect analogy, but few are. You know, however, that **if you do nothing, you won't catch any fish or buyers.** If you don't have a rod and reel, or net, or bait, or aren't at the right place, you'll catch no one. Meanwhile, the pond, lake, or ocean grows larger, not smaller.

There are thousands of fishing rods (tools) today, great minds churn them out daily. We also have our own skills and talents, computers, software programs, apps, the Internet, automation, and AI. Technology makes it possible to reach and capture hundreds of millions of people.

However, like most roads to success, you must be systematic. Or darn lucky. But luck, even prayer, rarely pays the bills. Organizations, businesses, and governments exist for decades, then lose market share or power and disappear.

What pays the bills is the right action, at the right time, for the right audience. That's sustainable growth.

Attract attention

How do you attract a stranger's attention?

Just say, "Hi there! What about those Phillies last night?" or "Let me get the door for you," at Wawa. Or a well-used greeting in New Jersey and New York, "How ya doin'?"

Catch someone's ear or eye. A smile, a wave of your arm or hand to show you're normal, polite, even cheery. Most people, unless in a rush, respond or stop.

You do this daily. We live, work, and play in neighborhoods, high-rises, villages, farm towns, cities, or offices. In a thousand places we run into each other. It's similar on the Internet too, with Facebook Likes, Comments, posts or emojis. Everyone has views, loves, wants, and needs. People are much more open now to receive such things from strangers.

You are in business with one chain-linked goal: sell your services or products, pay your bills, make a profit, survive, and grow. With 8.4 billion babies, children, youth, adults, and elderly on this planet, you and your business are trying to attract one or more segments of that population.

How? With a personable "Hello," in your voice, ads, brochures, everything. **Literally or figuratively you "Open your mouth." It's an exchange. For example, don't hand out a business card, ask for theirs and swap.**

Imagine playing catch with a friend. They expect you to toss the ball; you expect it back. You and your business are trying to catch attention because you hope they are receptive, looking for you, or for the "ball" you offer, a product or service.

But every one of us is bombarded with 4,000 to 10,000 "balls," or advertisements each day. We ignore most. We only 'catch' the funny, odd ones, clever ones, believable ones, or colorful ones. Those we haven't seen before catch our eye or ear because they're new. <u>Or, most importantly, we find them pertinent.</u>

"Appearances are everything." We need to look normal and reasonable for others to trust us. "Normal" has to suit the audience we are trying to attract; and it can't be fake. **Your customer's perception is your reality. You exist as their trusted friend. If your actions don't match your words and media blasts, you'll lose trust.**

Human networking is in our DNA—making connections and relationships is what life is for. We are social animals in human skins.

When I was 15 in 1965 selling magazine subscriptions door to door at my first summer job, a smile meant entry into a stranger's home. It worked because people wanted to hear more and see my samples. A few teenage girls home alone also invited me in. We partied and… well, 'nough said.

Sales requires two things: building relationships and providing what people like or want. Build relationships by:
- catching attention and being yourself
- smiling and being friendly
- being trustworthy
- finding common ground
- exchanging information

Your goal is to reach a special tipping point: instant recognition.

Humans share more in common than we do in outward differences like looks, ethnicity, education level, backgrounds, politics, or country of origin. We are one race, human, not 4 or 5 or 1,000. You, as a person with a business, want and need to connect with thousands of your "cousins," or maybe you only need five great customers. It's no secret how to make their acquaintance and become friends.

First, overcome your own hesitancy. Be hopeful and knock on their door. Second, open your mouth. Smile and talk. Show your best side. You are the best networker ever invented. You know best what it is you offer.

The very best and first way to grow your circle is to bring your friends and family on board. Ask them to help you.

You have a wide circle of friends and email and phone numbers. Maybe hundreds of friends on Facebook and social media. Ask them to review or promote you or complete a quick survey on Google Forms or SurveyMonkey. Put a one sentence Bio and your photo or logo on your business email signature.

Cultivate their interest in your new business. When they spread the news about you, business will jump. They are your promoters and influencers. This is big and exciting news! You've opened a business! Don't be shy, broadcast it!

Chapter 19 Principles of service

Chester says: ***It's long been the Age of Service and only businesses that provide top service will make it.***

Whatever your principles and views, as long as not violent, there's room for you and your business in free societies.

We live, work, and play in a service-based world economy. In 2021 the services sector contributed 77.6% of U.S. GDP, Gross Domestic Product, and 63.97 Global GDP. (Statistica)

Services account for most jobs. Everyone needs services from and by people to produce, manufacture, package, or deliver hard or soft goods. Direct service providers like plumbers, hair stylists, pharmacists, drivers, engineers, carpenters, lawyers, accountants and on and on have added importance. That means online services too. Covid, Zoom, and telemedicine proved it.

R

As a contract negotiator for the State of New Jersey for Information Technology products and services, I sat across from suited salespeople from CA, IBM, Oracle, Cisco, Microsoft, and dozens more. Their contracts were worth millions. It was tempting to promise we would sign the agreement to get desired discounts. But after my first big procurement I learned the reality of business.

I could only promise what I had authority over. I had no control whether the State Director of Purchase & Property would sign the contract I laid before them, or if they'd balk at it. That taught me to be above board, have my ducks in a row, be compelling, and follow through. In 30 years, not one requested signature was withheld.

Everyone depends on something or someone for approval. Few of us are generals that order armies and battalions around. You can't force a potential customer to click a "Buy" link. But you can make your product or service attractive, have compelling offers, and show success which draws more sales.

The goal is: reach those with the ability to approve. That means entice them, convince them, and have them buy what you offer. "Close the sale."

Sales aren't sales until cash is in the bank.

Like Wimpy in the old Popeye cartons and his promise to pay on Tuesday for a hamburger today, unless you intrigue or convince your target audience to click "Buy" on your sales page, purchases will be bleak.

You must *show* the public they need or want you. Telling alone turns people off. Authors like me know that well. "Show don't tell," is sage advice. Take it.

Your goal is not to be Walmart with 10,500 stores. Your goal is to pay bills and salaries and earn at least 20% in profits as you grow from 1 to 10 to 100. When you gain the public's eye and trust, you'll expand.

Your reputation is the only thing under your control. It's your foundation and major means of influencing buyers.

What makes great service?

Treat everyone as a VIP. If you give great service, folks will flock your way.

Service is being helpful and honest. Service is timely, fair, positive, knowledgeable, capable, and courteous. It's understanding and patient, even when paid just $2.75 an hour. That was a waiter's or waitress's minimum wage in NJ until raised to $5.26.

Think about the great servers you've had at restaurants or diners. On a return trip, you might ask for them. Good tips rely on personality and good service. **Customers pay more for excellent service and come back.**

You'd think twice if your server was curt, rude, slow, unkempt, or got your order wrong. You'd revise your tip downward, maybe badmouth the establishment. **Negative reviews reach and turn off others quickly. Excellent ones garner praise and attract others.**

Paycor.com shows U.S. state minimum wages at https://www.paycor.com/resource-center/articles/minimum-wage-by-state/ **As a business owner, you need a salary higher than minimum wage.**

...rvice

...e beginning of the Modern Age in 1760, humanity has ...versed the Age of Enlightenment, the Industrial Age, the Machine Age, and the Nuclear and Space Ages. Now it's the Information Age, and part of the AI Age. **These ages fit under 'Service.' Today, service distinguishes who we are.**

Wikipedia says we are in a "product-service global economy," the "servitization" of products. Even the venerable behemoth IBM, who exploded this IT Age with bleeding edge data processing in the 1960s, labels themselves "a services business." I wish I had bought shares in 1968 at $230 each when I followed Wall Street in Economics class.

The more service-oriented you are, the greater your success. Copy from great examples.

R

Working for the State of New Jersey, I dealt with dozens of personnel and staffs in technology companies and government agencies. IBM and Microsoft stand out.

In 1972, I was a mainframe computer operator for the Treasury Department. The IBM 360/40 mainframe I operated was bigger than three refrigerators, and had 256 Kilobytes of magnetic core processing power, only one-fourth of one Megabyte. Input was thousands of punched data cards for COBOL applications.

An IBM Customer Engineer, Mac, a handsome young bachelor, was on our raised computer room floor almost daily if it we needed a repair. IBM's office was nearby 3 long blocks away. That's support.

Since then, as a Windows user and fan, with online help, like IBM did back then, Microsoft has saved me from my own errors and cyberattacks. Their Support is 12 on my scale of 1 to 10. Hardware OEMS helped too, like HP and Dell. Warranties even provided machine replacements.

Great Operating Systems (OS) that run billions of consumer computing devices and millions of businesses are only as good as their designers, system analysts, system programmers, and coders. iOS by Apple is also top-notch.

Today, society and business rely on people, computing, networks, systems, and service. Service must be top-notch to match product quality and reliability. Poor service equals disgruntled users, hurts processes and sales, results in negative reviews, and Chapter 7 or 11, or a takeover and sell-off.

What business takes

Chester says: ***Business takes vision, passion, smarts, determination, agility, flexibility, learning, personality, and decision making. Above all, Action.***

It takes purpose and hutzpah to run like a demon in a track meet and throw one's legs high to clear the hurdles while charging top speed toward the finish line. You are that hurdler, running and overcoming barriers, competing with others, and dealing with demands and surprises, even a shoe that falls off.

You must practice the qualities you most want to be. **This is who you are, your reputation, the only thing you take to your grave. Your business reflects you like your website does. Both are mandatory in this modern world.**

Stay neutral, but…

G

Over the years, we at the Chesterfield Learning Center tutored dozens of home-schooled children. Their parents had either discovered they weren't prepared to tutor their own children in every subject, or they couldn't tutor them in challenging subjects such as physics.

Some parents wanted us to evaluate their children either through tutoring them for several lessons or giving them a diagnostic test. **Since nearly all our students came to us after**

school, being able to tutor students during our off times helped increase our income.

Most home-schooling parents either sent their children to a religious academy part time or used conservative curricula. Since Ilene was Jewish, and I was more of a Unitarian Universalist (if anything), **we put aside our biases and accepted the students for the sake of the business.**

All of one young girl's writing assignments included a reference to God or Jesus. One day she showed me a picture of (a white) Jesus and quoted the Bible verse Matthew 14, saying, "You of little faith, why did you doubt?" For her, Jesus's walking on water was as believable as seeing a hovercraft do the same. **I bit my tongue, as did Ilene.**

We joined two religious-based home-schooling groups: one based in Richmond and one in our county. Over the years, a few members of the group contacted us to test their children to determine if they were on grade level.

Out of curiosity we attended a conference in Richmond sponsored by one of the groups. We were surprised at the scope of the displays: One company displayed battle axes, swords, and other multiple kinds of weapons in defense of the Lord.

We felt very uncomfortable in that environment.

If you feel uncomfortable or something's wrong or may go wrong down the line, trust your instincts.

Help others

If you ask, "How can I help others," you will do well. You started with an idea or vision. You opened a service business to fulfill that vision. You made a Business Plan to express that vision (covered in Volume 1). Now you've dedicated time, energy, and resources to it.

Grow and succeed by adhering to the **Unity Principle. Say**:

"I will only achieve the growth I seek with unity of thought, vision, and action in me and amongst my staff, team, partners and clients." **Everyone appreciates help and assistance.**

As you proceed further through this book, take out your Marketing Plan and update it. Part of it will contain steps and resources to lead you to growth. As you go through this text, set specific targets to obtain growth and sustain it. Get out your colored sticky tabs too.

Chapter 20 Buyers and Sellers

Chester says: *Put it in writing. Be courteous and respectful. Don't speak or write to others when angry.*

All business, commerce, and most human transactions start with an Offer to Buy or an Offer to Sell.

R

Every person is a Buyer and a Seller.

Since 1960, J. Wellington Wimpy from Popeye the Sailor cartoons pitched everyone he met with, "I'll gladly pay you Tuesday for a hamburger today." Wimpy was offering to buy, on the poor credit of his name, a hamburger.

Today, companies adore and love the millions of Wimpy's who sign up for their "free" trials and get their "hamburgers" with a tap or credit card. Automatic renewal, of course.

As a buyer yourself, you should look for trials first before shelling out payment for something you need. Customers look for trials too, that's why so many sellers offer them. For a seller, it's a foot in the door to someone's wallet or purse.

When anyone—any person, any company, any organization—puts out a sales advertisement of any kind, what it really says is "I'm for sale and you can have me (for a price)."

It's an offer to sell, described in a few words or images, at a given price for a definite time. It's a promise to provide some physical item, or someone's expertise or service to help solve a problem, or to be entertaining in return for payment.

When Wimpy, or you, accept that "hamburger," you become a buyer. Commerce is trillions of hamburgers.

> The vast numbers of offers are offers to sell.

Services are hot. They sell like ribeye or filet mignon hamburgers on credit. Services in the U.S. are 16 <u>trillion</u> dollars, by far the biggest segment, sold at an astonishing rate. At 3.9% unemployment, there are millions of jobs for everyone. **Buyers, sellers, government, products, services, and jobs make the merry-go-round of world commerce spin.**

Today the world runs on Services. *Fifty years ago, it was manufacturing and mechanical industries, but we've automated those.*

G

We assumed that all checks written to our business would be honored by our bank. However, a check for two hundred dollars bounced. We contacted the parents of the young man we had been tutoring. They told us to resubmit it, but again it bounced. We finally threatened to take them to court.

Within a few days, they delivered cash to us.

You are the Seller. You need to be paid, sometimes partially in advance, or after providing the item or service. But in retail sales, it must be before they walk out the door or click offsite. Transactions are instant.

If not, invoices should say something like: "Net 20, 2½%". The Net 20 means the buyer has 20 days to pay. The 2½% is the interest charged when late. You set both, but 20 days is the minimum most companies use.

> *Don't threaten to take someone to court or get a collector unless you back it up and go through with it.*

Understand your buyer

"What do buyers want?" Well, what do people care about? The traffic, weather, their income, themselves, their family, jobs, and their health. What do care about? Everyone has priorities too, which fluctuate.

There are billions of products and millions of services to choose from. What makes a buyer buy? Why do we buy? You know because you've been a buyer and a consumer since you were a babe. **We buy whatever fulfills a need, want, or desire for someone or something.**

Biologically, two intrinsic natures make us "human." An animal, or lower nature—our physical bodies and its drives for water, food, clothing, and shelter—and a human, or higher nature—our intellectual, emotional, and spiritual sides. We try to satisfy both aspects. We prioritize based on circumstances, abilities, and resources. **What marketing does is create an urge to buy. That urge overcomes obstacles.**

Strangers will look at what you offer and go through a split-second or a prolonged thought and emotional process before clicking "Buy" or tossing that envelope in the recycle bucket. Same on any Amazon, Shopify, Etsy, or Walmart link. **Every buyer is looking for a solution. Not always to a problem, but often. Business provides solutions.**

Shoppers go to a retail store, or an app on their phone, a website, or Google search. When they find a match or a thing close to what they want, they instantly ask:
- Will it work for what I want?
- Do I like it? Will it satisfy me?
- Will this cost a little or a lot? Do I have the $$?
- How soon can I have it?
- Does this look legit? Is it a reputable source?

It happens in seconds. If your website sales page answers these questions well, the shopper clicks "Add to cart," or "Buy." However, impulse buys can override questions if in the right mood, the right moment, and the right circumstances. Sellers love these; that's why store aisle displays cost $$.

All buying questions reduce to two:
Will this benefit me? How soon can I get it?

Always answer both questions.

Laws and agreements

R

No one knows all the laws. International, national, state ones, and the Uniform Commercial Code (UCC) which has codified standard offers to buy or sell. The UCC contains appropriate language for bills of sale, forms, etc. Every commercial transaction between buyers and sellers is a legal contract.

A contract
- is an agreement between two or more competent parties (persons or entities),
- contains mutual promises to do a thing or to refrain from doing a thing which is neither illegal nor impossible,
- even if verbal, agreement results in an obligation or a duty enforceable in a court of law.

In this online world, everything, even the apps we use to buy with every day, are based on an agreement. Facebook, Google, YouTube, Piggly Wiggly et al., have Terms of Use and/or Terms of Service, even if free to join, or, if licensed, both.

For example, in 1980 I "bought" a 99-year Perpetual License for a software product for our Treasury Department IBM 3084 mainframe computer. You can't buy software that way now. It's licensed or subscribed to each year. You don't own it, the company/seller does. They have exclusive rights over it. You get a non-exclusive right to use it.

> *In Offers to Sell, sellers set the terms.*
> *Buyers agree or not, as in retail sales.*

If you want the app, product, service, or whatever thing it is, you must "Accept" the seller's terms. Don't accept, and it is a NJ Turnpike highway exit. Especially retail sales unless you're at a flea market and dicker over a cash price.

From patents to proprietary rights to copyright laws, **sellers set the rules.** That's the biggest advantage having something that someone else wants.

Use this to your benefit. Wait for a sale when you want to buy. Couponers like my wife are famous for that, and deals or specials overcome $$ roadblocks. I once mulled over the purchase of a software license of ProWritingAid for $200. It went on sale at $125 for a Lifetime license. I jumped on it. **Buyers can ask sellers for changes, discounts etc., <u>and should</u>, but only the seller can change their own terms.**

> *You will sign agreements to run your business.*
> *Study their Terms carefully.*

Government and business are the biggest issuers of Offers to Buy. Thousands of agencies, departments, divisions, or offices buy directly from vendors. Get on their vendor lists. They are online. You must jump through hoops to win the award, and the process takes longer, but it could be lucrative.

Elements of contracts

R

You are selling your skill(s), time, and expertise. Therefore, you need a contract with your user, client, or customer.

Ignore Optimum, T-Mobile, and others who trumpet "No contracts!" They are lying. They have Terms of Use you must abide by, which automatically apply when you sign up.

If you offer complex services, go to a lawyer to draft yours up. Most lawyers handle business, criminal, or personal issues. Use one that knows both personal and business law.

Service agreements must be simple clear language. Show:

1. **The Offer.** "I will perform…."
2. **Acceptance.** What constitutes a satisfied customer?
3. **Mutual Assent.** A meeting of the minds.
4. **Capacity.** The law assumes the parties have the capacity of mind and legal age to enter the agreement. Minors cannot.
5. **Consideration.** What thing of value ($$) is promised between the parties?
6. **Legality.** Parties cannot enforce a contract in a court of law for illegal services or products.

Agreements can be simple. But without all six elements they are not usually upheld. If one party does something, the other must reciprocate.

Your business can offer services anywhere in the world. In the U.S. your state is your "nexus" and sets the rules for your business, enabling you to sell. Your home or a building must have a physical address. You must comply with your nexus state's laws. National and interstate laws are administered by the Feds. **Laws vary by country and state, so know those that apply to you, especially taxes.**

"Contract" is not a dirty word

Protect yourself and your business. Contracts, Terms of Use etc. do that. Get it in writing.

"Contract" is not a dirty word, it's a protection. A contract between two or more competent parties is based on mutual promises. A product will perform as advertised or someone will provide services as described. As buyers, people accept these two conditions without thinking hundreds of times a day.

The reason consumers don't like contracts is that they only protect the company and limit company liabilities, which causes distrust in buyers. **Regardless, civilization hinges on one word—Agreement—a social contract.**

Every minute, someone like you offers something to sell in an ad, on a business card or website, on a retail site or through merchant services. You contact someone; you talk or email or text back and forth. You both agree on what, how much, and when to start. You perform, deliver on time, and are paid. You issue a receipt and record the transaction.

Both parties are satisfied, the contract is complete.

Your texts, emails, or documents are the legal contract. **Verbal agreements are worthless. They are wide open to disputes.** Contracts and Agreement Ts & Cs are for avoiding miscommunication, missed promises, and disputes.

A customer accepts your terms, or you agree to modify them. If not, walk away. You need to protect yourself and your business.

When purchasing items or services, no Google, no Facebook, no social media accounts, checking accounts, hospital services, home rental or mortgage, no employment, no offer to sell can go unaccepted without something written if you want what they have. A receipt alone is proof of a mutual transaction.

Signing up online for a new thing? Downloading a software program? Unless you sign, initial, or click a small "I Agree" box first, they won't sell it to you.

Understand anything you're signing, or what you want a customer to sign. Only what's printed or shown on the document matters.

Protect yourself. Agreements have indemnity and liability clauses for that. Have a Standard Agreement and negotiate specifics for services to be performed. <u>No agreement can cover every contingency.</u> Your company is legally bound by anything you sign or accept. Don't leave performance dates open-ended.
Every business knows it's harder and costlier to sign up new customers than it is to keep current ones.

Retaining current customers is cheaper and easier than making new ones.

Offer customers a deal or discount to stay. Cable companies are notorious at that. Cablevision offered me a $50/month bill instead of $150/mo if we didn't switch.
Big companies have standard agreements. They merely shrug if folks don't accept. Once accepted, it's tough to find discounts after the initial enticement and sign-up. Another bon mot is that most U.S. vendor agreements mandate that any dispute go through the American Arbitration Association.
Products are generally sold "As is," or have a parts and labor warranty or extensions for a fee. There're lemon laws too. If you get stuck somehow, your county Small Claims Court may help recoup up to $3,500 in disputes.

If you sell services create a shell legal agreement you can modify and use with each new client.

Service Agreements

R

In 2013, for my editing business which served individual writers, I composed a two-page agreement shell. It has stood me well with tweaks and additions for publishing as well. Tweaks include specific requirements for the client or job. A Sample of my editing terms are in Appendix A.

Sample language and templates for legal documents are available from LegalZoom.com, Nolo.com, PandaDoc, Rocket Lawyer, FindLaw or others for a fee. Modify yours in MS-Word, Pages, Adobe, or Google Docs and tailor it to each specific customer.

Adobe pdfs have an eSign capability, as does PDF Architect, and DocuSign, so you can both sign the same document online. Adobe also has a pay feature. Electronic signatures are legally accepted. **Only ever send final agreements as PDFs.**

If you "drop" your services agreement on your client without notice, expect them to balk. Be up front about it, send it early and ask them to review and comment. Change what you must, even charge more or less. **In small business, "negotiation' is key to growth. But do not begin services until the pdf or printed agreement is signed and countersigned.**

Chapter 21 How to sell

C*hester says: Eve sold Adam the apple and look what happened. There may be a steep price on love, but when we want it, well….*

Two kinds of purchases

When you pay a shopping bill at Acme, Shopify, Wayfair, or Walmart, the transaction is complete. Whether you bought only a quart of milk or an Amazon Cart full of books, you pay based on each item's price, that is, a One Time Charge, a OTC, at that moment in time. Most retail goods are a OTC. Services can too but are usually paid in increments.

Sales bring profits, either on the unit cost or in volume. **But the gold standard of sales is recurring profit.**

Acme wants me to return and buy milk and other stuff again. That's a kind of recurring sale, an iffy one since I can run to 7-Eleven for milk just as easily. Multiply that scenario by millions, hence competition. **The best kind of recurring sale and profit is a subscription, and sellers know it. Building up Rewards and cashing them in is another.**

Hook the buyer on the product or service and have them automatically renew annually, quarterly, or monthly, like magazines, software, or HVAC inspections etc. Notice how hard it they make it to cancel. Advice: Call to cancel a renewal; you may get a discount.

"I vant to suck your blood...."

Paying a One Time Charge is like Dracula draining your blood in one gulp. Signing up and paying a subscription is like Olivia Rodrigo's vampire boyfriend sucking blood from your veins drop by drop over periods of time. Like Amazon Prime at $14.99, or a Washington Post sub. Make sure:

 1 you use the product/service often or a lot
 2 benefits outweigh the costs

Maintenance and updates, newsletters or reports, repairs, support, and warranties are popular subscription schemes. **Subscriptions are part of the Monetization of Everything.**

For example, if your customer balks at renewal, offer a discount or gift as incentive to renew. This should be an automatic pop-up as a customer is about to click away from the site. Or in the 2nd renewal notice.

Types of selling

Google "the types of selling" and over 20 pop up, like solution-based, transactional, consultative, and provocative. We are familiar with wholesale by selling items in bulk and saving on packaging, shipping, and delivery. We know retail best, in any store whether a physical place or online, where the price is marked, take it or leave it.

Today sales are lumped as either B2B or B2C. No matter the selling method or means or come on. There's an interaction between customer and seller, or if online, a linked platform.

The basic process of selling has 7 steps: prospecting, preparation, approach, presentation, handling objections, closing, and follow-up. Study these.

A step might be skipped or shortened but the end is payment and delivery of the item or service product, whatever it is. Books on how to sell, famous and popular, even pithy abound, as do sales techniques. Zig Zigler's *On Selling: The Handbook* comes to mind, and Dale Carnegie's *How to Win Friends and Influence People*. There're many specific ones. Read.

Upselling

The greater the income they have, the more likely buyers are to buy. Smart marketers and advertisers always push for higher sales or the next sale. They upsell. They want to milk a captive audience or buyer, whether in their store or online. Look at how Amazon and the others offer *Other items you may like*. **You should too!**

Upsell anyone with incentives, like McDonald's does and every other food chain, with Combo Meal Deals. It saves a buck on the combination but earns them more on the total dollars spent. **Upselling is two Fish Filets for 6 bucks or adding another at a discount.**

It occurs at ordering or checkout and generates more revenue. It includes marketing more profitable services or products.

Think outside the box. Act outside the box. What are you really selling? What else can you sell? Automated tools make it easy online to offer more and upsell.

In sales, more costs less. Making 2 and buying 2 costs less than 1 doubled in price. Volume discounts have been around forever. Buyers expect them, so give them options. Note how many subscriptions offer 2, 3, or 4 "Plans" to add features.

Or the other guaranteed sales ploy: the multi-year deal. "Sign up for 2 or 3 years now for big discounts." Every firm loves this, especially software vendors. It means bonuses for salespeople, more income for the company over a longer term, and makes it harder to leave the contract.

Packaged/discount offers attract us because we think we're getting more for less. We should know better, because the deal is only a good one for as long as we use the item. Coming back never guarantees the same deal.

What's your buyer's budget?

R

During my career with New Jersey as a contract negotiator, meetings with a new company's sales reps had one common goal. After polite introductions and a brief presentation, before talking product price, they pointedly asked, "What is your budget?"

The answer tells how much someone can or will spend. Once shared and a sales rep knows it, they meet that amount or stretch it, offering perks or discounts to seal the deal. Or they upsell.
You want to know your buyer's budget.

When negotiating price with a buyer, ask their budget so you can sell to it. Offer multi-year plans, discounts, subscriptions, contracts, or memberships. They are the epitome of recurring income, called "evergreen contracts," because they renew automatically.

In blind sales, the income demographics of your target audience show possibilities. Get that from the platform you advertise on.

Pricing

You set a price, and buyers consider it. Therefore, decide what your price represents before you set it.
   Value and quality, YES   Satisfaction, YES
   Timely completion/delivery, YES   Profit, OH YES

Profit is income made that exceeds the costs to produce, market, sell, distribute, and deliver. In most cases, sales taxes are added. You decide how much profit you need or want, but that's less important than why.

Visibility, Branding, Volume, Personal Wealth, or something specific are all good reasons. Determine the "Why" first, and the amount to charge for your services is easier to determine.

"Surge pricing" meets high demand, such as paying for added employees, or higher costs for materials. "Dynamic pricing" is similar, and with microsecond wireless AI interfaces, prices on any digital sign or menu can be changed in seconds at any moment. Airlines, hotels, Uber, and Amazon use it, and Walmart and Kroger are going "dynamic." Expect more.

Look at what competitors charge for the same or similar services. Decide to be in that range, lower, or add value to your service and charge more.

The "Why" is critical in any ad campaign. The "What," or price, is critical for achieving profit. Offering services, that means earning what your time and effort is worth, such as more $$ for speedier completion/ delivery. It can fluctuate.

The "How" you sell comes later and is ever-changing because of technology, the economy, and market forces. I once consulted with Kiki, a NJ SBA advisor. She looked at my website and service prices. She came back and said, "Double it, you're worth more." It didn't hurt business.

Margins

We hear the term "profit margin" in business. We recommend 20% minimum. You'll hear that a lot from us. It's not a hard number and fluctuates depending on the specific sale, ad campaign, pricing, the audience, or discounts. You, as owner, marketing director, salary earner, bill payer etc. must set profit margins.

First, consider the "Cost of Goods Sold," a common expense category. It's the direct costs of producing the item or service sold in terms of materials and labor costs. If you buy a woman's purse for $30 (the "material"), and resell it for $40, your cost was $30 and profit $10. Your services costs may include rent, materials, or supplies and hourly rate or salary.

Second, determine the breakeven point for items sold or services provided in dollars, equal to the cost of goods sold.

Third, know the purpose of selling. Is it strictly promotional and there's a small loss on price? Or a lower profit margin to boost brand recognition? Is it a special sale or limited run like a holiday sale hoping volume brings profits?

Whatever type it is, monitor sales and monitor profits.

Recurring revenue

"Passive income" is income from recurring sales like subscription renewals, affiliate marketing, or from steady customers. **It's the easiest income to make—you already have the relationship.** They like you, your products, services, information, or the arrangement, and they stay with you.

You've earned trust and confidence. It's the only kind of win/win that will make you successful. <u>However, businesses can only grow through new sales and recurring revenue, both.</u> It used to be called 'repeat business,' but it can come from many sources, like affiliates or even investments. Subscriptions are a big kind.

Never take current customers for granted. Work as hard to retain them as you do to acquire new ones.

It is easier and cheaper to retain a customer than to acquire a new one. Buyers want choices and savings. You want their cash, credit, loyalty and trust. Costs to acquire new customers rise because customers are savvier and have more choices. They can leave quicker. Today that is the fate of every poor servicer or poor product. It's like advertising tycoon David Ogilvy said, "Good marketing helps a bad product fail faster."

You must have good products and services. Monetization of Everything means if there's a way to charge for something, it will be found. Once, photo sites like Flickr and Pixabay were free. Now most everyone charges by tier, plan, Pro, or Premium features. Multiply those thousands of times.

Nothing wrong with charging for what you do!

Today, information is a commodity the same as loaves of bread on a grocery shelf. NPR, Wikipedia and Wikimedia accept donations, they must survive. They have equipment, staff, software, and a headquarters to pay for. So do you.

If we don't pay for what we like, it will disappear.

The monetization of Everything means if it used to be free, someone now repackages it and sells it. If it costs little to create, someone still pays for it to be available and maintains it.

G

We offered volume discounts at the Learning Center, like ten one-hour tutoring sessions for $420 instead of $450, at $45 per hour each. Payment was always in advance, and we offered weekly or monthly contracts, too. That way, we had the funds up front. Bundles were very popular.

Next to new sales, longer term recurring income is the sweetest. It is the backbone of any business. **Work hard to satisfy and retain repeat customers.**

Chapter 22 Finances

Chester says: *If you can balance a checkbook and are nice, you can run a small business.*

<u>Imperatives:</u>
Stay in business by running it smoothly
Earn enough profit
Be great with people. Treat them well.

R

Your nexus state applies the rules you must follow, as do the Feds. Technically, once formed, you only do two things to remain in business: file Annual Reports with your state and pay taxes, mainly income and sales.

The annual report is due on the anniversary of your formation and is about $100 for an LLC. **Most states now require, and only provide, online filing.** Following regulations and reporting requirements is a pain, but they've increased because industries proved they can't be trusted to self-monitor or self-report. Or correct glaring deficiencies or alter bad practices.

Reporting for an LLC is not difficult. The IRS and states provide examples. With tax software, accountants, articles, the internet etc. anything you need is available. It really is just balancing your checkbook. The formula is:
- Statement Balance
- Less uncashed checks or items outstanding
- Plus, deposits made since Statement date
- Equals actual (checkbook) Balance

Keep the balance in the black, not the red, and thrive.

Use professionals

R

It's daunting to figure things out yourself, but that's how we learn. **When professionals are necessary, hire them.**

My wife and I have long used Joe for our tax returns, and he uses a tax prep product to file with the Feds and state. We use Craig for our financial assets. Young, savvy, and responsive, the first time we met he compiled a detailed binder of our assets. Helpful. Hire a CFP to manage and grow assets and investments. As fiduciaries they act in their client's best interests, not theirs. Fisher Investments has the right attitude.

Janet and I have had trusted lawyers since 1980 when we wrote our wills, Power of Attorneys, and Advanced Directives. Getting all three costs $500-$1000. Look at GoodTrust.com for help, samples, and estate planning. You need to protect and care for your assets, especially if you have children, or your state will decide for you and your heirs.

Don't forget technology. Your smartphone, computer, and Internet are assets critical to your business. Look for Legacy planning setups in your accounts and emails, which provide a fallback if you don't use your accounts for 3 months or more. Assign a designee to manage them after you die or are laid up, or at least save or transfer the data. Have an Advocate who can speak for you when the time comes, and it will.

Don't die without a Will (intestate). Don't let your State distribute your personal and business assets.

G & R

Like RREnergy before it, Rod's ABLiA Media started with $1,000 in a new business bank account, a bank credit card, a home office, PC, Internet access, an All-in-one printer, and a smartphone. And a brain and fingers to type and create. A salary wasn't expected until well-established.

George and Ilene's Chesterfield Learning Center started with a $90,000 home equity loan because it needed more startup capital for leased storefront operations, store renovations, cubicles, and computers etc., and later, paid staff.

ABLiA began with no expenses for computers, salaries, rent or lease, utilities, water, or paid marketing materials and advertising because they were sunk costs; already there. The Center started out obligated for those and much more.

A day and night difference.

But regarding finances, we both had the same concerns and had to know or learn enough to stay organized. Areas are:

Funding—money to build a good brand name and reputation, and for assets to start and grow the business
Revenue—income from all sources, especially recurring
Income—from sales of products, services, and other
Expenses—costs to start and run the business
Cashflow—income less expenses on a daily basis
Profit—income less expenses for a given period/ activity
Budget—projection of income and expenses for the year
Taxes—Federal, state, county, or city

"In the black" is profit; "in the red" is loss or debt.
- **Accounting** enters and tracks numbers and transactions
- **Bookkeeping** records transactions, invoices, receipts and keeps statements
- **Audits** check for weaknesses and recommend improvements or corrections

A business may need an accountant or CPA to tie ends together, or a tax preparer for filing federal and state tax forms annually. Or use a semi-automated accounting software product like Quicken, QuickBooks, HR Block, Intuit TurboTax, TaxSlayer, TaxAct or others yourself. They are all online. You provide the data and file online returns. Watch out for them pushing high-priced products. **In millions of small businesses the principal or owner does it themselves.**

You'll always need funding for startup and ongoing operations. Funding comes from your pocket, investors, revenue from sales, or lenders. You can crowdfund also.

Budget your business

No matter size or scope, businesses share common income and expense categories.

R

Every business budget an estimate of monthly or annual income and expenses based on its calendar year. Make one 30-60 days before the beginning of the fiscal year. I estimated my first ABLiA Media budget using an MS-Excel spreadsheet, good enough for a small start. Budget categories can vary, depending on your industry.

ABLiA Media LLC first year Budget:
Jan 1 – Dec 31   <u>Opening Balance</u>   1000
<u>Income</u>
   Services   500
   Books sold   600
   Other   100
                Total   2200
<u>Expenses</u>
   Salary   0   (TBD)
   Mktg & Advertising   400
   Cost of items sold   200
   Materials & supplies   50
   POB, Postage & shipping   50
   Website & software   400
   Dues & subscriptions   100
   Training & conferences   250
   Phone (**)   0
   Travel & Transportation   30
   Printing   60
   Other   60
                Total   1600

<u>End of year Balance</u>   600

The first years are meager until earnings exceed goals. Breakeven is the minimum, but only lasts for a while.

Mistakes I made were not setting written sales goals or marketing goals, nor methods to reach them, and not taking a salary. Those were colossal, colossal errors.
  A Business Plan and Marketing Plan avoid those errors.
  Budgets examine the economy and the year ahead. In tough economic times, there is less discretionary spending, i.e. less disposable income or $$ not obligated to committed expenses. Cutbacks or layoffs may be necessary.
  Tight times are tough, bad, or the worst possible for any business or individual, as I and my first company RR Energy & IT Consulting found out as part of the aftermath of the 2008-2009 Recession. I even retired in 2009 through a buy-out.

Tough times require a loan, cutting back, using savings, or dissolving. Look at Covid. Office leases plummeted. Layoffs galore. Businesses shuttered. People died.

  In downturns, government revenue and programs suffer, the labor force shrinks, and incentives die. We all suffer when public services are cut back.
  By law, some State Budget's like New Jersey's must remain balanced throughout the year, i.e. total expenditures must not exceed total revenues. **The federal government doesn't care.** National debt is 34 trillion dollars. It increases every minute with interest and new borrowing. We are a house of cards.
  But that's impractical for businesses. In our personal lives, with credit cards, access to loans, etc. we Americans spend more than our income, like $1.13 trillion just in credit card debt in 2023. That's setting up for a huge collapse of trust. You could use a Debit Card system, like Found.com.

Move $$$ between budget categories, or show losses for a time, but businesses and governments must show a positive balance sheet or fold.

If government isn't stable, businesses won't be stable, and life, society, won't be stable. That is a tremendous worry and concern. The runaway train must be stopped.

G

We opened our Learning Center in 2012, and a storefront opening, "a launch," needs physical furnishings, equipment, and preparation. Business launches are a great opportunity to get the word out, both to the press and invite the press, officials, friends, and many others, advertise, and make it special.

Here's an after-action report of expenses we tallied for Chesterfield Learning Center Inc. for 2012:

Accountant	$400
Tutors	$475
Insurance	$425
Furniture	$3,600
Installation of cubicles	$1,500
Used chairs	$350
Lease deposit	$2,000
Woodlake monthly newsletter	$650
Computer and 10 reams of paper	$1300
Lowes hardware to improve center	$205
Walmart television and stand	$655
Reimbursement to ourselves	$14,400
TOTAL	$ 25,960

Starting out, besides the lease payments, we knew that learning center cubicles and computers would be our biggest expense categories. Once startup and onetime costs were paid, we'd have a more manageable monthly nut to crack.

After some years it was obvious our small business was well underway since we also recouped some personal funds we had originally invested. That gave us hope to continue.

Midway through our third year of business in 2014, we could pay off the rest of our debt to our family who had helped us purchase our house, and to reimburse ourselves for the money we attained with our home equity line of credit.

This was a turning point, for we could stop worrying about debt and also be able to increase profit. We were smarter in knowing when and where to advertise and to ignore sale pitches that promised results but gave no evidence of other companies attaining them.

It takes 2-3 years to become profitable, on average.

We did not raise our rates, nor increase the salaries of our employees, but we encouraged patrons to consider long-term commitments to tutoring. If parents paid for ten lessons in advance, we charged $420 instead of the customary $450. Saving just $30 was enough to entice clients to pay for "reservations" of specific tutoring days and times before anyone else could grab them.

By the end of our fourth year, after no longer having to pay one rent payment for our new place, and one for the old as the lease expired, we finally began reimbursing ourselves for the home equity line of credit.

You need to account for the numbers. Its critical for taxes and reporting. Use accounting software and get used to it. Consult an accountant or CPA as needed.

The importance of reporting

Every corporation (C or S) must maintain a Balance Sheet by quarter and year of total Assets, Liabilities, and Equity. Assets are cash and equipment. Liabilities are bills to be paid, debts, or loans. Equity is stock held by the company or shareholders. The Balance Sheet is made public. Wall Street stocks jump or plunge on these reports. Two other major corporate statements are the Income Statement and the Cashflow Statement.
 However, the LLC is a company different from a strict corporation. LLCs don't have shareholders. Reporting rules are simpler. An LLC doesn't have to publicly reveal a Balance Sheet because it's private. **For an LLC, formal government "reports" may not be required, other than filing state and federal taxes.**
 Using an Excel ledger, ZohoBooks, or QuickBooks, make it easier to prove that accounts are in order. Any taxable entity can be audited. **An LLC owner/ sole proprietor is 100% responsible for the business, even though, like a corp, personal assets are protected from legal suits.**

Chester says: No matter the type of business, maintain a balanced budget and you'll succeed. Keep good financial records.

 When tax bills go unpaid, it's a recipe for disaster.
 For the sole-proprietor, if "running the business" also means "being the business and doing all the work," you'll falter like the Titanic after smashing the iceberg. Without pacing and balance, you'll run yourself into the ground and kill the business. **Say "No" to work you cannot deliver.**
 According to a Forbes article, the IRS statute of limitations for auditing is now only three years, but sometimes they go back further. **So, keep W-2 and 1099 forms, orders, receipts, and payments for 7 years.** Keep receipts for renovation or remodeling projects. If itemizing on your tax bills, you can claim depreciation. **Only receipts, bank transaction statements, or documented payments back up your claims.**

Keep good records and stay on top of it. Balance your time between duties, customers, and your private life.

The Ledger

Al Capone's secret ledger "book," obtained by the Untouchables and highlighted so vividly in the 1987 movie, sent him to jail for tax evasion when nothing else did.

Now it's QuickBooks, Google Sheets, Netsuite, Sage, or others. **When starting small, you only need a few things. A Ledger is one. An Excel spreadsheet can be enough to start.** When larger, it can be ZohoBooks for $15/mo or another.

Keep a ledger by 1. Balancing bank, credit card payments, PayPal transfers etc. every month, 2. Only entering completed transactions, 3. Showing and receipting all income.

At a glance, your ledger shows: Beginning Bank Balance
plus, all Income (Deposits)
minus all Expenses (Payments/Withdrawals)
equals Ending Bank Balance for Month or YTD

Record deposits by date and source, and expenses by line item, amount, and date. Have two columns for deposits—one for Income from sales, and one for Other. Put expenses in their own category, column, or bucket. Entries must agree with the bank statement. PayPal and others have statements too.

Quickbooks is the big name out there for semi-automatic accounting software, and it has many versions and interfaces. It's expensive, around $42/mo for a small business they told me. You have to call them for a quotation to even get a price, which tells you something.

Look into cheaper ZohoBooks, Xero, Wave, Sage, or OneUp. Some are specific functions like Striven for inventory or FreshBooks for freelancers. Many have desktop vs. online versions.

R

I was treasurer of my Baha'i religious community off and on for 34 years, and my bookkeeper wife Janet helped me balance my books with five accounting tricks and more:

Tip 1. At the start of each Fiscal Year, give each deposit slip a number starting at 1 from the first one. Number the receipts deposited with that same number. This way, receipts, and deposits match. Accounting programs do this automatically.

Tip 2. The Rule of 9. If adding up a group or column of numbers and the difference between the result and what's expected is a multiple of 9, it's likely the digits of two numbers are swapped or written wrong.

Tip 3. Parentheses (__) around a number means it is the opposite of that column's meaning.

Tip 4. Never enter a negative number, i.e. a minus sign - .

Tip 5. Never "change," posted entries in the ledger. Enter an "adjustment" on a new line to correct errors. Paper entries must be in ink, not pencil.

Chapter 23 Banking

Chester says: *There are thousands of physical or online banks and places to keep $$, or transfer it. We can spend it or collect it instantly.*

R

A few people may hide their cash under a floorboard or under a Serta mattress. The rich may hide it in the Cayman Islands. Everyone used to carry more cash. Coin shortages come and go, and pennies might be eliminated.

Remember the bank run on the Bailey Brothers Building and Loan in *It's a Wonderful Life?* **You need an FDIC insured bank to store your funds. At least you'll recover up to $250,000 if the bank fails.** There are 4,300 banks with 72,000+ branches insured in the U.S. They have rentable safe deposit boxes too, but those aren't insured.

Modern digital banking services rely on one main ID: your email address and SS#. Those and a password grant access to accounts, Auto Bill Pay, EFT transfers, savings, CDs, investments, their own debit/credit cards and more. You can make check deposits with a snapshot on your phone.

Banks are using ATMs and digital to replace tellers. Bankers are "Advisors," are fewer, and you need an appointment.

Choose a local bank branch you can reach easily.

The biggest American/International banks with 13,000 branches alone are Chase, Bank of America, Wells Fargo, and Citibank. **You could go totally digital with one of them or Capital One, Ally, PNC, Chime, Found, Varo, Synchrony or Discover etc. but check pros and cons.**

Only call the Customer Support or Fraud number printed on your monthly statement, or on the back of your card, not from an email or letter. It could be fake. Never react to anything emailed to you from an unknown source or an unknown caller.

My daughter received a letter mailed from Bank of America. The letterhead and its red square logo, and the text, looked 100% legit. The letter said it need to verify her account and gave a number to call at once or the account would be closed. We checked the number given against the Customer Service number on her last printed bank statement.

Bogus. We didn't call, we reported it.

Getting paid

R

It used to be "Cash is king," especially when haggling over a price at a garage sale or flea market. It still is, it's just digital. Even garage sellers accept phone payment apps. My author book sale apps are tied to my bank, and that's where I'm paid my royalties.

Nothing else is as important as getting paid. You want to get paid by customers and others fast. Digitally is fastest.

Accept credit cards and digital payments via Square, Payment Depot, Stripe et al., or through PayPal, Apple Pay, Google Pay, Venmo or others. Start out with at least one.

EFTs, digital transfers, and Direct Deposit are regarded as legal and safe.

The beauty in 2023 is that a banking app on your PC or smartphone can handle an in-person debit account or credit card sale or payment. I pay for my WAWA and Dunkin' coffees with apps on my phone. Likewise, so do Merchant Services or FinTech apps online or from your website, phone, or anywhere else. Found.com, Novo, Karat or Oxygen are full-service online banks, with invoicing, tax management and more.

It is expected or a requirement that you have digital processing as a seller. The beauty is this works to pay bills, receive or transfer funds, and more, and account for it.

Use Direct Deposit or Payment

Years past there were wire transfers, now called digital transfers. Like bookseller royalties for authors, automatic direct deposit into a bank account takes effect quickly. Check writing and mailing etc. is costlier and slow; only older generations may do it. Literally, take a photo of a check, send it, its deposited.

If you use pay bills directly from your bank account, get Alerts when payment is due, then paid.

Banks are great. Transactions post every day. Set an Alert for when a withdrawal is over a set amount and get an email notice. Likewise for Balance changes. **Any company, service, or vendor that transfers $$ into your bank accounts must have a tight, secure network.** Alerts are protections.

Include your bank's fraud number on speed dial on your phone. The quicker you catch fraud, the more you salvage. Credit card companies and banks have responsive 7/24 fraud services and charge dispute services.

A general rule is: if you call them, they can ask for identifying information. If some stranger calls you, never give yours out, no matter where they say they're from.

If you write checks, don't use blue ballpoint ink. It can be "washed" or erased by thieves, rewritten, and cashed. Use a gel pen with black ink.

Everything is digital/online/automatic. Companies and Government mandate it. ***Do not fight it. Embrace it.***

Chapter 24 Track your credit

Chester says: ***Credit is debt. It needs to be paid off. Avoid paying interest.***

Credit cards or accounts started in 1934 when American Airlines first issued its Travel Card, with 15% off for flyers. And they really "took off." Now no one can afford <u>not</u> to have access to credit and cards. A FICO score indicates credit worthiness, and 35% of it relies on payment history. Over 90% of lenders use it to check credit worthiness.

There're a million cards, well, hundreds. Don't pick any based on perks, rates, ease of use, or features. Pick it based on the upstanding well-known bank that feeds its transactions.

Commerce has always depended on credit. **Credit is only maintained with a belief you will pay it back.** Legally it's a loan. That's the contract you make. Minimum payments prove you are reliable but cost interest. Credit card issuers love interest. **But don't give it to them.**

> *Keep all that love to yourself. Pay in full and never pay interest.*

You'll have expected and unexpected expenses. Don't fall into unnecessary debt. Pay back on time if possible. Nice words, but they can differ from what was first planned. But if you monitor your income and expenses, and that 20% profit level as you should, or use debit only, you'll never pay interest. **However, credit sure comes in handy when you need an umbrella for a rainy day.**

Businesses and box stores have their own cards, called "store" cards, backed by banks like Citibank or JP Morgan. Big banks set policies for the Big Four—VISA, AMEX, Discover, or Mastercard. The Big Four and others love to sign you up, receiving $133.1 billion in paid interest and fees in 2022.

Refrain from opening more than a few card accounts unless you use a store often. Just using a card adds a hidden 3% onto the price. And all items get priced higher to cover it. **Cash Back Reward cards have a "Swipe fee"** that stores must pay to the card issuers, which they hate and hurts their bottom line.

No matter which card you use, save cash by paying off the balance when the statement comes. Interest charged can be 29.99% on cash advances. **Paying interest on cash advances, credit, or debt is stupid unless unavoidable. Interest paid is income you've wasted and opportunities lost.**

Your credit history determines how easily you'll get credit. You need one primary and one backup card for physical and online purchases. Use Credit Karma, NerdWallet, BankRate.com, or WalletHub to find and compare deals. One card may be VISA or AMEX, so get another well-established one like Discover, Mastercard, or Capital One. Sign up with an online application and get instant approval with a good credit score and history. Avoid any annual fee.

Apps on your phone use a card, and online purchases require one or access to your bank account. Dozens of cards have low introductory interest rates. Avoid variable rates. Keep a list of every vendor account you have a credit card with or has access to your bank account in a file drawer, locked.

Keep business accounts separate. Never mix with personal ones. Like they say, "Keep business (oil) and pleasure (fire) away from each other."

Enjoy your business, yes, but be smart.

Using credit

Chester says: **Credit cards might be the biggest legal scam ever invented. Who doesn't need to pay "over time" on occasion. But 29% interest is a waste.**

G

As soon as we became Chesterfield Learning Center corporation, Ilene and I discussed how to open a checking account for the business. We didn't know the ins and outs of running a corporation—we were new. We wanted to use a different bank than the one we used for our personal accounts so we could keep our finances separate.

First, we obtained a home equity line of credit, made easy because we had no mortgage, and placed those funds into a new business account with the same bank. We had good personal credit ratings, so within two weeks of applying for an account as the Chesterfield Learning Center, we gained approval and received business checks.

Every month for a year, we added money to our business account from our personal account, writing a receipt to ourselves, having faith we'd pay ourselves back. Near the end of each month, we used a large whiteboard at the back of the office to do our figuring, and being naïve, we always projected that all we needed was a certain number of students to sign up to succeed.

But we also realized it would be a long road until we paid back the loan. At first, we had so few students their parents paid with checks, but soon a man came into the office and introduced himself as a marketing agent who offered a credit card system. By that time, we had obtained our own credit card for the business but had no system for accepting cards from others.

Know your monthly expenses. Include annual ones. Estimate your income needs every month, especially for payroll. Stay on target.

John offered a way. He explained that **credit card processing fees** were paid on each card transaction, and we would pay:
- an interchange fee went to the bank that manages the credit card,
- an assessment fee went to the card network such as Visa,
- a payment process fee went to the company that managed the system, the one for whom John worked.

Each transaction would be charged 2.5% of the total, which we thought fair. The next day, John came back with approval for our use of the system and a machine that accepted credit cards. Every month we'd receive an accounting of transactions.

Few carry checkbooks now. Use merchant services to accept payments credit cards etc. electronically.

Within a year, we also accepted credit cards on rare occasions when someone signed up for lessons who had spoken to us during a venue event. Ilene handled the transactions using Square, a small physical device she connected to our iPad. This worked well, because although we reluctantly accepted cash, many clients still carried checkbooks.

Based on amounts transferred digitally, Like PayPal et al., two deductions may happen: a transaction fee of a few cents, and/or a percentage charge. If you invoice someone for $100 on PayPal or Square, they pay the full amount, but you'll receive a few dollars less in your bank account.

There are dozens of merchant services providers.

PayPal, Square, Stax, Stripe, Chase, are a few who do it for around 3%. Compare reputations and fees.

R

Future transactions will only be digital and have digital receipts or records and no one will print or mail paper. Everyone is stopping mail and paper. Even my bank ATM sends my deposit receipts by email. Credit card transactions are all digital.

How you buy matters. You have apps on your phone that automatically replenish funds directly from an account or credit card. Billions of items and most software programs are purchased/ subscribed to online. Companies want online credit card payments used for what they sell, or PayPal etc. whether monthly or annually. In fact, they demand it.

Watch closely any vendor credit card account with a recurring monthly or annual charge. Adobe's huge suite of products abounds with monthly charges. Make sure you fully utilize a vendor's products or services; otherwise, cancel them. RocketMoney.com checks for that.

Every company wants cash directly deposited into their account at the point of sale. It eliminates "float," and they get paid quicker. Only use business credit cards or business accounts for your business, whether online or off. **Never mix business with personal purchases. Never.**

Use cash or a Debit card at the Point of Sale and avoid interest. Do not use your browser's automatic field filler for credit card data. It takes 10 seconds to enter. Don't let your information get stolen from a tracker or by a data breach.

Get a receipt from vendors, email or otherwise. Print or save digital ones to digital file folders. Keep a manilla folder by fiscal year handy and put bank statements, deposit slips, and receipts in it. Keep a separate one for credit statements.

When paying an invoice, record date, check # or credit card used, or account, and amount paid. Use a good All-in-One printer to print your statements, receipts etc., scan business documents, or email them from the printer.

We're in The Digital Age, also the Age of Transition. What Tim Berners-Lee began in 1989 as the World Wide Web was lightning in a bottle. It exploded. Compaq, HP, and IBM/Microsoft made it universal via Ma Bell and AT&T. Now it's a supernova with Artificial Intelligence.

Credit cards are the tip of the iceberg, 2-5 in every pocket and on phone apps. **We couldn't subsist without credit cards. The most important way to choose a credit card is to vet the bank that the cc uses.**

Safeguard your credit

Make sure your credit card company has robust fraud detection and good dispute resolution. AMEX is best.

Track and protect accounts:
- Copy your credit cards and ATM cards front and back and stash the copies in a secret spot.
- Note those vendors you use online cards for. Include your phone app accounts too.
- When using a credit card or Apple Pay, PayPal, Square, or wherever, make sure they provide statements and are archived. You'll need to print them for audits.

TransUnion, Experian, and Equifax track credit use and rate it. Each keeps its own FICO score accessible for a fee. MyFICO.com is out there too. A score of 740-800 is Very Good. Get your free information at https://www.experian.com - no credit card required. You can get it from Credit Karma, but they ask lots of identifying info.

Improve your FICO Score: Pay on time, even if minimums. Ask for higher limits. Canceling cards lowers scores. Don't open tons of cards.

You can refuse to give your SS# to credit companies, banks, doctors, or anyone, <u>but they may refuse you services.</u>

Anyone can pay a fee and pull your Credit Report. Companies have standing procedures for that.

Consumers are paying $34 billion indirectly for credit card fraud because store owners and companies raise prices and rates to make good on losses. So, don't cry. It's laughable how lax we are with our apps and swipes, and careless about receipts. Store clerks, gas jockeys, etc. don't even offer them unless you ask. **Watch out. Money is money in whatever form it takes.**

Don't let anyone steal yours.

Use cash

Cash has comeback for good reason; it saves money. Offer cash for a discount. Shops and service people offer cash discounts. We don't use cash like we once did. If we did, we'd save the 3% hidden tagalong fee built into every credit card purchase. On $100, that's $3.00. Multiply that by the dozens of card purchases made each day or week. No wonder AMEX, VISA, and others have billions in profits.

And from the 29% interest they charge on partial monthly payments.

Credit is a two-edged dagger; Always carry a credit card, but do not waste good income on paying interest.

Some like me run on Dunkin'. Society runs on credit.

Chapter 25 Backbones of business

Chester says: ***To become income it needs a receipt. Expenses need a paid invoice.***

You prove income was received by issuing a receipt and physically depositing that income into your bank or other fund account unless done electronically; expenses need invoices from the vendor and apayment entry. That's how to prove income and expense transactions. The IRS or any taxing authority only trusts and accepts legitimate records, including bank statements and credit card receipts.

However, a paid invoice does not prove that the expense was an "ordinary and necessary" business expense for IRS purposes and tax deductible. This is crucial when filing taxes and in audits. Paid invoices, receipts, and statements "back up" your story when you do claim income and business expenses. Accounting, bookkeeping, and ledgers deal only with the recording of transactions.

Invoicing

Q. Do I need to invoice for my products?
   Yes. Your sales page, order, or checkout page does that.
Q. What about when I sell my expertise, skills, or time?
   Get a signed agreement or issue an invoice first.

Bank statements are actual transactions backed up by orders and receipts.

You need a written invoice when someone wants your services. It could be by email or other written means. Include:
- Who from (Your business name)
- Date
- Who to (Client or customer name)
- Quantity, item, service, or job description

- Unit Price, Rate, or rate times hours
- Discounts
- Sales tax if applicable
- Total due

Selling services is not similar to selling products because services are provided over time. The length and terms depend on agreement between the parties.

Whether you realize it or not, every order page is an Offer to Sell and a potential invoice as well. Take ordering on Amazon, for example. When you add an item to your cart or just click "Buy," you've agreed to the description, price, delivery, etc. That's now an Order/Invoice. Payment concludes the transaction, which include the policies of the seller. The paid order/invoice becomes a receipt.

This is why your order/sales page is critical to get right. Your checkout page, or someone who does it for you, such as Merchant Services, collects, and confirms customer invoice and payment data and executes the purchase.

Remember: online payments hit your account quickly. A receipt or confirmation needs to be issued. If online, it can be printed or emailed. **A survey by Freshbooks of 1,000 diverse business owners showed 65% of them used digital billing, invoicing, and receipting.**

Save and issue receipts

Everyone on Earth is a buyer and a seller.

When buying coffee at Starbucks or anything anywhere, you're asked if you want a receipt. **That's a Bill of Sale, or transfer of property. It's a legal record.** Make sure you get one.

A Bill of Sale or receipt proves to the IRS or taxing authority that an item or service was exchanged and paid for. They are critical in disputes. **Every business must somehow offer/give receipts. Yours too.** If smart, you'll save them when you buy something. You must save them for your business, whether you

buy with cash or credit. Especially credit. **Credit card receipts are crucial in audits too.** Receipts show:
- name of issuer/seller   date/time, maybe location
- quantity and name of the items, and cost
- sales tax if any   total paid
- how paid, cash, credit, etc.

A receipt proves the transfer of ownership from a store to you. A receipt from a service vendor means a part or the whole of the service has been completed and been paid, which also means acceptance of the work.

Whether selling directly or indirectly, issue a receipt. It's proof of new ownership.

For online sales, transactions are electronic, like using PayPal, or by tapping "pay" on your phone app, or by entering a credit card. EFT transactions are recorded in a vendor account, under your name, instantly. For purchased or licensed software apps, receive an automatic instant email with an order/ receipt number, product name, price, expiration date, or download link.

Use timely tools and resources

R

Discipline means training. Train yourself on available online tools and programs or hire others. You don't need 10,000 hours to master it. **Every master was a disaster at one time.**

The backbone of business is the Internet. It's hundreds of millions of sites and billions of links, most of them old. Search results can be sporadic, and paid ads show first. Or fake ones.

You'll create a ton of documents with MS-Word, Apple's Pages, or Google Docs. Scrivener, WordPerfect, or Calibre. ProWritingAid, Autocrit, MS Editor, Grammarly etc. edit and proof them. Many software programs are complex, multifaceted, with millions of lines of code and tons of features.

As a writer, I always draft, edit, format, polish, publish, and share in MS-Word. For tips, I subscribe to Alan Watts WordTips at www.wordribbon.tips.net and Microsoft's Kevin Stratvert's Word Tips on YouTube to learn.

Find and use experts for your industry niche, for the Programs you use, and tasks you want to perform. Many are free. Coursera.org, Alison.com, Khan Academy, Udemy, and others offer free to audit or paid classes on everything. Use HubSpot Academy for great marketing info.

Train, train, train. Set a training budget. My six figure career with the state was only achievable because my department had liberal training policies.

When searching out data, only use a recently dated version of information that applies to your PC system, application, business, or goals. Look for the month/year date on answers you seek or in articles you read. It would help immensely if every published item, article etc. was dated, but they're not, since the vast majority is outdated.

Once you find a trusted site you use often, hit the "star" in your browser's top line and save it in Bookmarks.

Use Google's Search qualifiers found here: https://support.google.com/websearch/answer/2466433?hl=en#

A search on the Internet brings up a half-million "results." Finding your exact answer, company, product, link or whatever, is finding a needle in an ocean-deep, blue-linked Mariana Trench. **Never forget that search results could be false or phishing. Beware, beware, beware old search results.**

Reinvest from profits

Put money into infrastructure, marketing, employees, training, and debt retirement. They pay off and are part of the umbrella for rainy days. Don't forget insurance: liability, product, and professional. Check SimplyBusiness or NextInsurance.com.

Chapter 26 Death and business taxes

Chester says: **From ancient times, death and taxes are certain. But taxes shouldn't scare you to death.**

Make time to do the right thing, and the thing right. No worries that way. When done, it's a very pleasant feeling. **When it comes to business, documentation talks and BS walks. Hypocrisy, lies, and cheating get folks caught and ruin reputations along with trust.**

Taxes are our legal obligation. In return we should get security, benefits, civil society, and services. We earn the right to live, work, or run a business in America.

Income taxes

R

In the U.S. the Feds and states tax personal income. Essentially think of it this way: <u>All income is taxable unless specifically excluded.</u> When your data is organized, it's easy to use fillable form programs to file online with IRS Free File, Intuit TurboTax, H&R Block, TaxAct, Jackson Hewitt or others. Millions do. Tax prep companies and CPAs are up-to-date on the latest regulations.

The U.S. government imposes income, business/ corporate, capital gains, and other taxes; states do likewise, and sales taxes; municipalities mostly rely on property taxes; some cites have wage taxes. If a business owns physical property, taxes are due. Federal taxes apply based on the form of the business, or structure, declared on IRS Form 8832. Capital gains as well.

On the federal level, adults and businesses file income taxes based on a progressive system. Earn more, pay more.

Income from wages, salaries, sales, commissions, bonuses, tips, investment income, and certain types of unearned income and more is taxable. Tax brackets for individuals range from 10% to 37% until 2025. Regular C corps are taxed a flat 21%.

However, the amount those ranges are based on may change. The infamous March 15 or April 15 deadline. Individuals with their LLC data file a Federal 1040 long form and a state 1040. There are standard deductions or itemized deductions and tax credits. S-Corps and partnerships file on March 15.

Where I live in New Jersey, it's called Gross Income Tax. States have their own tax tables, rates, credits, deductions, etc. Both federal and state rely on the individual filer's status, such as single or married to determine status and bracket.

If collecting Social Security too, check www.ssa.gov for info on earning limits depending on age and income.

You should have a Social Security Administration online account for sure. Also, login to SSA Business Services Online at https://ssa.gov/bso for info. Social security is part of our lives from when we first start earning income until we Americans receive a lousy $255 check for dying and coming off SSA rolls.

For your business, you may file under your SS# or if you have one, simple to get, an IRS Employer ID, an EIN.

Business taxes

Legitimate businesses only exist at the behest of the IRS and the state they form in. To continue to legally operate year after year, businesses must pay taxes quarterly and file Annual Reports with their state. **Generally, business taxes on business income are: income less allowable deductions, plus any tax credits or incentives**. The feds use a "pay as you go" system. Taxes are calculated, due quarterly, and paid online. States are similar.

Unfortunately, all taxes and rates aren't fair and too many loopholes serve the rich. Some wealthy Americans pay no taxes or little, big businesses too. Because our government overspends on defense, pet programs, and congressional Christmas tree deals, U.S. citizens are drowning under 33 trillion dollars of debt holding our breath.

Individuals and small businesses are caught in the middle because we can't afford high-priced tax law firms to find loopholes. **However, to legally operate, tax returns must be filed and paid when due or there will be penalties, even wage or other garnishments.** You can fight City Hall but not cheat it.

> Most businesses and organizations are required to file "information returns" with the IRS, — Form W-2, a 1099, and others — when they pay you. The IRS matches their information to your tax return. That's how they catch you if you underreport.

Single-member LLCs, which you may be, are considered "disregarded entities" by the IRS. As an LLC, you can file annually as part of your 1040 Individual Personal Federal Return and declare business Profits or Losses on Schedule C.

But don't be fooled by its simplicity: documentation requirements are onerous when you read the instructions, so keep backup. LLCs can elect to be taxed as a sole proprietorship, partnership, a C-corp, or S-corp, so it's flexible.

State Taxes are filed and paid online using your account on your state's website. If you owe a federal tax of $1,000 or more quarterly, use the IRS EFTPS system. **File on time to avoid penalties.**

Penalties are a supreme waste of your precious income.

Pay strong attention to allowable deductions before filing any tax return. Check annual law or rule changes.

Sales tax

R

There is no federal sales tax, or VAT tax, yet. If there was one sales tax rate across the nation and prorated income appropriated to the states, maybe. State Sales and Use Tax collections must be remitted quarterly. Five states have no sales tax: Alaska, Delaware, Montana, New Hampshire, and Oregon. Find yours at https://www.usa.gov/states-and-territories.

Commercial sellers with a U.S. nexus must collect state sales tax if applicable. For your products sold on retail sites or stores, they collect and remit any sales taxes to your nexus state directly. **It's great they do it. You don't have to worry about it.**

For my past professional consulting services as RREnergy, or now as ABLiA Media, there were no NJ sales taxes on professional services. **But on most physical items sold, and certain services, sales taxes must be collected and remitted.**

When I sell my books from the trunk of my car, it's tangible property. I collect and pay sales tax or pay it from what I charge. **When selling an item for cash, never charge cents. Always round to the dollar.** Do you really want to carry change around to break a $20?

There are "small seller" exemptions for those selling to customers in states other than their own. Check your state.

Federal and State personal income taxes withheld from wages during the year appear on W-2 forms, Wage and Tax Statement, sent out by the end of January. You can deduct state and local sales taxes instead of state and local income taxes from your IRS 1040, but you can't deduct both.

Technically, taxes aren't taxed twice. Deduct paid taxes. Don't include sales tax to calculate your tip at restaurants or anywhere else.

Stay ahead of tax changes if you don't have an accountant. Visit IRS.gov and also subscribe to your state's business website and/or its Division of Taxation or Revenue. Sign up for newsletters and tax updates.

Learn the rules and filing deadlines. Common sense and following them keeps cash in your account not theirs.

Know what applies to your business, and what doesn't. If you can't figure it out, consult a tax adviser.
Become familiar with Federal form 1099-MISC, used to report your payments to independent contractor or servicers, or payments to you. You issue them in January for any prior year's payments and must send a 1099 to the provider. There are 17 types of 1099 forms. **Good records save you in an audit.**

The States and the IRS would rather not collect penalties for late tax payments. They'd rather your $$$ was used to pay applicable taxes on time when due.

Employee taxes

Whether self-employed or not, based on business entity type, you may have tax liabilities. Some municipalities register businesses too.

If you have or hire employees, businesses must pay Federal income and employment taxes, less allowed deductions, or credits. That includes 50% of their employees FICA, which helps fund social security. There is unemployment tax too, among others. Check rules at IRS.gov.

Self-employment tax

Federal self-employment tax is collected from self-employed individuals and small business owners who don't otherwise pay withholding taxes on salaries or earnings on Federal 1040s. They may be sole proprietors, freelancers, or independent contractors who carry on a trade.

The tax is about 15% of regular income, but half may be tax-deductible. Even if collecting SS benefits, you may have to file Form SE with your 1040. Estimated payments may be required.

Credits and tax deductions

Google "business tax deductions" and "tax credits" often since they change by year. Credits reduce the amount of tax due; deductions reduce the amount of taxable income. **Not all business expenses are deductible.** These are some:

- Startup costs   Advertising and marketing
- Taxes, fees, interest, and charitable donations
- Travel, mileage, meals, entertainment
- Retirement plan contributions
- Office supplies and furniture
- Professional services fees
- Education & training   Certain software
- Wages & payroll taxes   Bad debt
- A home office   Insurances
- Utilities   Rents and leases

NerdWallet has info on this for 2023-2024: https://www.nerdwallet.com/article/taxes/tax-deductions-tax-breaks Pay attention to federal (IRS.gov) and your state's defined expense deductions, incentives, tax credits, and rebates. For example, there are those related to energy, like electric vehicles, solar, etc. **Don't assume what's deductible; verify it.**

Solopreneurs working from home may think they can include house expenses because that's where they work, but that's false.

You must measure the square footage of your exclusive work area and only use that.

IRS.gov defines deductions in Publication 535. "**To be deductible, a business expense must be both ordinary and necessary.**" An ordinary expense is common and accepted in your industry. A necessary expense is helpful and appropriate for your trade or business. **At the federal level, businesses can carry over operating losses indefinitely.**

G

Ilene and I had learned from our attorney when setting up the corporation that paying taxes for our tutors made a difference whether they were full or part time. Our tutors were independent contractors, so we did not have to deduct money from their checks, but we had to issue 1099 forms at year's end to show income paid to each of them.

Chester says: *Businesses fail when they shouldn't. Not just because owners and/or staff can't operate the business well, but because they avoid bookkeeping and record keeping tasks or get overwhelmed by them.*

Some businesses fail because the principal is not only doing the work, but also selling and marketing, keeping "the books," scheduling, etc. and does all tasks poorly.

If cash flow is poor, if expenses or staff salaries must go unpaid, if government deadlines are missed, or if you can't pay off debt, try a debt reconciliation service. Some are free. Consultations from these agencies help, especially in reducing credit card debt. But watch carefully if they charge.

There will be surprises almost every day in any business. React promptly to resolve them.

Remember: The feds and the states want you to succeed, not fail or pay penalties. And your customers do too.

If you are not good at accounting hire someone part-time who is. My wife Janet's earnings as a travel agency bookkeeper helped pay for her college degree. If you hire an accountant, they should be a CPA.

Businesses rely on a stable government, we all do. Government relies on taxes. Without fulfilled mutual obligations there can be no stability.

Here's the famous quotation we remember from Benjamin Franklin, in a letter to Jean-Baptiste Le Roy, 1789:

Our new Constitution is now established and has an appearance that promises permanency; but in this world, nothing can be said to be certain, except death and taxes.

Ben was a brilliant statesman, first Postmaster General, an inventor and more. We must pay our share, businesses also, but this saying has changed. Taxes are decreased or evaded with sharp accountants and lawyers. Death is not as early as it once was with our longer life expectancies.

When prepared, don't be scared.

Chapter 27 Only 18 hours in a day

Chester says: ***The place we work should be ideal for focusing on priorities. Manage the time you have.***

It started with the sundial in 1,500 BC. Now digital clocks that are much more than clocks exist on our wrist and phones. **Time wasted is money lost for the business.**

Time is our most precious commodity, hands down. We only have control over time available to us. That's 18 hours a day if we sleep 6, less mealtimes and breaks, errands, appointments, doctor visits, entertainment, relaxation etc. and you're down to 12. Oh, then subtract the hours you work on or at the business.

We can't hoard it like packrats, but we can be smart how we use it. **Automated tools help organize, prioritize, and save time. Selective ones are worth buying.**

G

During the first week of the learning center's operation in 2011, we visited the owners of the 19 other businesses along our strip. All were pleased to meet us, were receptive, and we swapped business cards. We all promised to display them in our offices.

The manager of the nail salon next door unexpectedly said, "Wait a minute" and disappeared to his back office. He returned with a massive appointment book, saying, "I hope you can use this." Ilene and I hefted the book and saw it as a good omen. If we could fill in lines with paying students, we would be successful in no time.

While the book was helpful for the first couple of months, we realized we needed a system that both Ilene and I could view both at the office and home. **Google Calendar rescued us.**

We developed assorted colors for each tutor, including ourselves, my student's names in blue, and Ilene's green. Since most parents paid in advance, at the bottom of each day's column, I typed in the amount of money coming in, minus the amount I would pay the tutor. Monday might be $285 and Tuesday $160. An average week was $1200, and that increased.

This was troublesome, though, for when a student did not show (or pay), I had to rework the totals. So, we also paid tutors $10 if their student canceled. It was unfair for them not to be reimbursed something for their downtime, although they used that time for preparing lessons.

Appointment Schedulers like Zoom, Square, or Calendly are a must. Sign up customers and meet face to face. Your website needs a booking manager too.

Do the work but…

Your greatest enemy is not time. It is not prioritizing it.
Do the most important thing first. Discipline yourself. Poor time management sinks thousands of businesses.

You may not enjoy doing this, but lay out your day, week, and month. Be early for appointments. Don't keep customers waiting. Use calendaring, scheduling, and booking systems.

Every morning, make or check your To Do List for the day, important times and events, appointments, and phone calls to make or emails to send. Set aside time for scheduling, to provide direct services, to manage, and time for yourself.

Part of a routine means keeping on top of financials.

Be reliable. Set aside time to do specific tasks and meet obligations during business hours.

When starting out on your PC, run a virus scan and check for Windows Updates. Run a Utility program like ASC, Glary, or Norton and clean out junk.

Manage the accounting, tax filings, and organizing. Keep a collapsing file folder: one slot for receipts, another for paid invoices and receipts received.

Make time to market the business or prepare materials, run ad campaigns, as well as monitor them. If working online, keep aptly named digital folders for digital documents.

Take breaks and know your caffeine limits. Mine is 6 a day. And please eat. Take 10 minutes and exercise or walk too.

Post on social media, your blog, or newsletter.

Set time aside to learn what's happening in your field. Google industry trends, marketing, or peruse news from SCORE, related organizations, and social media gurus. Educate yourself.

Sell face to face, even on Zoom.

Relax later with friends and family. Enjoy entertainments.

Warning: A life solely focused on the business will stress and break you and your family. Don't succumb to that life.

Organization skills bring balance and are your best friend in business, life too. **Your priority is to satisfy your customers and clients, to reach and gain more, and enjoy your labors.**

Prioritizing tips

R

When I first changed from blue-collar computer operator to a white-collar Information Processing career in 1980, I was a gofer. I didn't have to run for coffee for my boss but did everything else.

One task was to show the 16mm film by Alan Lakein, *How to Get Control of Your Time and Your Life,* to office groups. I ran that projector eight times. **I memorized how to prioritize projects A, B, or C, and how to prioritize—the 3 D's—Do now, Do later, or Discard.** They have guided me since, like focus, concentrate, and tackle the most important work or task first. Break big projects down and solve them in bites until done, like eating a foot long Subway hoagie. **Don't wait for a big block of time.**

In those early years, I learned to compartmentalize work hours away from the rest, live happier in both worlds, and not worry or be anxious. You must do likewise, or suffer. When I left work for home, it stayed there.

You may not get that luxury for a while, but that's the goal.

Beepers and phones can be a curse.

Broken promises

G

We assumed when people made appointments with us for tutoring, that they would show up at the center. But some did not. We often considered finding a way to charge their credit cards to ensure they would honor their commitment. We were not charging for consultations, so wondered why they would not arrive on time.

Since we had no negative reviews on the Internet, we deduced that a family member changed his or her mind, or that a less expensive tutoring business was found. Even after seven years of business, it still disappointed and angered us when we would drive to work for no reason.

So, we ended up only scheduling consultations when we discussed with parents the academic goals they had for their students. We encouraged them to bring in report cards and copies of the corrected papers. To make the best use of our time, we scheduled the consultations immediately before or after a tutoring session, or between sessions.

Clarify and Verify
Time is $$, costs $$, yet you can't buy time.
Don't waste it. Only 18 hours in a day if we sleep 6.

Chapter 28 Gods of the 21ˢᵗ century

Chester says: ***Inventors have been around since Man hit a stone against a rock to make sparks. Invention created machines, technology, AI, and runs society.***

R

This Information Age is a generation of the half-light, since everyone doesn't have modern computing devices yet, nor universal affordable access. **Untold inventions and human creativity created the newest god—Technology.** It affects all aspects of human life. It's composed of the holy trinity—Hardware, Software, and Networking.

Hardware, the equipment, like our bodies, is part of every computing and communication device, god the father. **Software**, the program languages, codes, and macros make up applications or apps, like our minds, god the son. Telecommunications, later **Networking**, is classed as the Internet and online everything, like hearing and speech, god the holy ghost. These three underlie modern civilization.

Add commerce and ecommerce, whom we already worship. Unless you run a completely cash-only business, you are ensnared in their viselike grips. These three technology gods affect how you run your business. **Modern business can't run without them. Ignorance in these areas will not equal bliss.** A smartphone, PC, or laptop is a must. We take them for granted—until there's a problem.

Online everything

We have problems truly grasping our device hardware, software program applications, and networking. They:
   a. Require intuitive smarts by the user
   b. Don't explain what their features or functions do or how they work
   c. May have poor, short, haphazard, or nonapplicable Help functions, knowledge bases, User Forums, or FAQs
   d. Show convoluted examples (like DOS commands)

  e. Show outdated problem/answer search results
  f. Are dumbed down with few explanations

Since Apple 1s appeared in classrooms in 1975, we became dependent on computing devices.

Software is king

It's not location, location, location, but software, software, software.

Software is a fixed annual cost, like word processors, virus protectors, utilities, graphics, and websites.

  Every reliable provider of hardware, software, networks and support for their products tries to make them foolproof. But complexities involved make that impossible when dealing with millions of human users of every age, intelligence, skill level, culture, language, and ability.
  Microsoft tries to provide clear, concise info on what its Windows products are, do, and how they work to their 1.4 billion users. MS examples of commands and settings are decent. However, Windows is based on DOS from 1981, then on MS-DOS from 1993. That's over 30 years ago!
  But technology never pauses. Microsoft announced costly Copilot at $20/mo, it's new AI, and AI is storming the capital.

As a business owner you need computing, software, and networking products and to know how to operate devices and browsers. They are investments.

  When you do not understand how your device works and functions, you become your own worst enemy. <u>You screw up your own device.</u> Choices are:
  a. Learn what you can, fix issues yourself, and save $$

  b. Use OEM HW & SW fee-based support or rely on third-party support to come up with a fix
  c. Use Utilities for efficiencies and effectiveness

 In the beginning, Data Processing equipment cost millions. Software was an afterthought. Then software got expensive, hardware cheaper. Then maintenance was charged separately for both equipment and software support. Today, customers can only "license" software by paying monthly or annual subscription fees. The subscription includes whatever technical support the vendor gives, and how.

It's always been Buyer Beware

 There are a myriad of software products, computers, and smartphone apps. New ones, even great ones, appear daily. Wait until they are battle-tested in actual users' hands and have honest reviews of both the product and the support before buying or licensing.

We users come last

On the totem pole of the best computing security, government and business come first because they pay through the nose for it. We home users come last, thrown to the wolves to decide what security software to choose.
 When we buy a new pc or laptop, we get whatever security product comes standard, like McAfee or Norton, but at least something is there, and should be. **Securing computers against cybercrime is a bitch, and costly.**
 Issues puzzle the techies too, let alone us. We rely on pc and laptop vendors to ensure the technology runs, and on software vendors to support us. **We pay for it, so demand the best. Call on them. Consider switching if they give lousy support.**
 Hacker criminals find new ways to penetrate defenses, get in deep, cause havoc, steal, and get away. Norton says 20% of

links redirect to a malicious link. There were 1,802 data breaches in 2022, over $422 million dollars impacted.

Even encryption doesn't prevent it. Nor does a https:// URL. Cybercriminals do anything, hurt any person, company, institution, national interest, anyone for $$$ or privacy data.

War, invasions, murders, violence and killing, civil unrest, invasions, pandemics, slavery, rapes, starvation, and natural disasters are bad enough. Civil society won't survive cybercrime too. **We depend on computers for everything and that's growing exponentially.**

Watch the 2014 movie *Transcendence* about the idealistic computer geek played by Johnny Depp and how they had to destroy all electronics to stop him. You'll get it. Now we worry about AI.

**Something must be done
or cybercriminals will destroy modern society.
<u>And your business.</u>**

Companies that make and sell hardware, software, and network connectivity are enmeshed in the middle of this cybercrime war we're deeply engaged in.

HW, SW, and Networking vendors try to make their products invasion-proof but can't. They've finally wised up and now charge for separate contracts or "subscriptions" to cover software issues, virus removal, system restoration, etc. like HP's SmartFriend. Others are jumping aboard this bandwagon.

One thing, out of the box, new hardware and software are safe, like that tower or laptop you just bought. But you must pay attention if you run a business yourself, from home or elsewhere. If we don't:

- become better educated,
- be more observant and avoid traps,
- verify solutions before changing settings,
- rely on virus scans, utilities, and user manuals,
- vet website owners and companies,
- increase security budgets,

- **and use two-step verification on all devices and longer passwords for accounts that handle $$,**

then we have shot ourselves in the heart, for the heart of our business will be crippled.

A great article on this is at Kaspersky: https://usa.kaspersky.com/resource-center/threats/computer-viruses-and-malware-facts-and-faqs

If you are a techie, use Belarc Advisor's Home version (free) and click "Security Benchmark Score" at the top. Expand the sections and red Xs show tweaks to make for tighter security.

Support at your fingertips

Thank goodness for vendor Technical Support. It, software or people, focus on fixes for problems in the hardware, Operating System, Programs or applications (apps), and networks.

Technology vendors have a support knowledgebase on their website with a search field of their articles, maybe a user forum, or a chatbot assistant, updates you can download, maybe a Help forum or email, maybe a live technician. **They all should.**

When it comes to browser support however, it's easy to leave Feedback, difficult to get responses. Forget live technicians. Google is the worst: they don't even respond to dire feedback. Try it, you'll see. But hey, Google is free, right? **To be fair, they have too many user issues to respond individually. They could offer it for a fee though.**

If User Manuals, or Guides, were standard fare, and came with all products it would help. https://answers.microsoft.com is a source for Windows and MS applications. Whomever the vendor, some answers are great, or pop ups outdated, are unclear, or inapplicable to the situation, like chat bots.

Frequently Asked Questions (FAQs), can be paltry, but check.

HW OEMs like HP and Dell have extensive equipment tests, with diagnoses and repair functions built in. It's like the Windows 365 MS-Word App, with a quick repair or full repair in Settings. **All software programs could be like that. I'm tired of techies that say, "unplug it and plug it back in," or "restart," or "uninstall and reinstall."**

Chat bots are limited. A live technician may be the biggest help. They can control your PC remotely, troubleshoot, and make software repairs, mostly by changing settings, or help with a system reset or full reinstall. **The problem everyone has is pinpointing a single problem out of all the complexities.**

There are few easy answers to HW, SW, and Networking problems. Therefore, learn what you can about your PC and its major components, settings, and aspects.

Time is the enemy. When our PC or Internet is bad or unavailable, we freak. We try clicking anything and damn the damage we inflict. Without a functioning internet connection, a user is supremely hampered trying to fix their device.

For this holy Trinity world we're in there's no full-blown user manual when you buy your device or program. Especially not for the "internet." <u>**That's why we users create so many darn problems for ourselves.**</u>

Many HW & SW OEMs have great phone or online remote support. MS Windows Settings has Get Help links, and System, Network, and Device Troubleshooters. If you have a repair contract with Staples Tech Support, the Geek Squad, or a local repair shop, maybe they can remove malware and fix or reset the PC. If the BIOS on the motherboard gets fried by hackers, the unit is worthless. Techs won't be able to save it.

Like everything, some things are repairable, others are not. If it's a corrupted browser, you're stuck until you reset or restore the system. There is no one to talk to personally at Google for Chrome. I don't know about Firefox. Microsoft may help with Edge/Bing; hard to tell.

<u>**In a word, browser support is pathetic to nonexistent.**</u>

The truth is ugly. In reality, we Users create or exacerbate the problems on our computing devices and in our networks.

Cyberpol

Cyber criminals are nameless, faceless, wealthy, clever, use advanced tools, and are insidious. They are masters at making the fake look and seem real. They play the odds and crime pays. They digitally siphon off boatloads of data, cash, or secrets from next door or 3,000 miles away, relaxing in the safety of their chamber. **They will not stop. They attack individuals, organizations, companies, and nations.**

Microsoft has a 74% market share for home and business Operating Systems and software applications like MS-Word, Excel etc. and has been hacked. Apple's 2.3b iPhones and 3.6b Google-based Android phones? All hacked. Companies, systems, individuals, institutions, and governments—hacked.

Everyone has their own security methods, software, programmers, management, techies, and internal support, e.g. nations, Wall Street or NASDAQ giants Oracle, CA, SAP. There's a plethora of cybersecurity products and standards bodies: IEEE, ICANN, ANSI, ASME, NIST, and ASTM. We have cybercrime investigators or chasers FinCen, Interpol, Intelligence agencies, law enforcement, HSI, FBI, IC3, CISA, and others. **As of January 2024, register your business with FinCen, the Financial Crimes Enforcement Network** at https://www.fincen.gov/money-services-business-msb-registration

All try to cut down attacks and catch criminals but are losing. It's well known the cybersecurity world is fragmented. Organizations fail to share information, IT professionals and C-level executives sidestep their own policies, and organizations banter their own cybersecurity lingo. **A 2018 study showed $600 billion globally lost each year. Every second, there are over 1,000 attempts at stealing or revealing data, let alone state secrets. Think Edward Snowden.**

Reporting an attack is haphazard, but in the U.S. go to:
- U.S.-CERT.gov (1-888-282-0870)
- FTC.gov or SSA.gov
- ic3.gov (FBI)

The world needs millions of things and trillions in funds to improve our lives and make us free and safe. We have laws and very smart people. Criminals are smart and clever too. Inadequate detection and enforcement are worldwide problems for every individual, business, and nation. **What we really need is one unified Cyberpol or CyberForce to marry expertise, intelligence, and technology to combat cybercrime.**

Chapter 29 Security doesn't exist

*C**hester says: **Making profits is #1. Protecting and guarding computing assets is #2.***

Because hacker criminals are clever and hide their program execution codes extremely well, your anti-virus, anti-malware detection software must be robust.

McAfee has a decent rep but may be simplistic. Windows Defender is solid as are Avast, AVG, Kaspersky, PC Matic, Malware Hunter, Malwarebytes and Norton. All offer multiple settings and scanners, with browser protection too.

The best thing you can do to avoid problems is to be observant as you use your device. Stop if something is out of the ordinary. Don't click an unidentifiable or unfamiliar link, checkbox, tab, or anything else, especially an http link. **The worst part of the computing industry is this: Vendors and anti-virus, anti-malware products only uncover threats they know about, not new ones.**

Run scans

Use your security product to run full virus scans of the C: drive at least weekly and run again if there is a question or you observe something off kilter. Scans check important rooms in your PC house. Utility Programs like ASC, Glary, and Fortect do too.

They can be a quick scan of key files, a System-wide one, or a Custom scan for a drive, folders etc. Found viruses will be quarantined. But frankly, they're hard to catch. The Windows

Malicious Software Program seems useless. But get in the habit of scheduling automatic scans.

Hacker criminals attack files, settings, browsers, email, and permissions. Protect System, Documents, Downloads, Pictures files, your browser, and email.

Passwords and security

Keep Logons and Passwords secret.

Your most important password is the PIN you set for Windows Logon. **Make it alphanumeric**. Write down past ones because if you forget your pin, Windows asks for the old one. Save email addresses and passwords. Google's can be the same as your Gmail account. Passwords are easy to change, but often hard to recover.

Dozens of Password Managers exist: NordPass, BitWarden, Dashlane, Keeper, and Sticky et al. LastPass had breaches recently. Most have special "Vaults" if desired.

Do not use automatic password fillers for accounts that access banking, online deposits or payments, credit card, or investment data, <u>unless you trust them.</u>

<u>Do not use AutoFill for bank accounts, credit cards, PayPal, Square, Venmo etc.</u> Password managers and auto logins are fine for accounts or vendor apps that don't use your credit card or have access to your bank.

Use a 12-digit alphanumeric password minimum for application program signons. Use strings of nonsensical made-up words, numbers, and symbols. One of my wife's was "Stupid3Pc." Don't use the same password for different sites.

<u>Use 2-step verification</u> for money transfers, banking, credit card access, or Merchant Services. <u>Choose between a text or email code to receive the code, text is faster.</u> Do not keep passwords written in your wallet or purse. Memorize your important logins, business, or personal email passwords.

It's risky using Wi-Fi Guest access hotspots, like at Dunkin, Panera, Starbucks etc. **so, don't. Do not enter your password.**

Get free ID Theft monitoring from AAA or AARP and be alerted of data breaches. If alerted, change your password. Better yet, change them every 3-6 months. Smart organizations and companies require it.

Do not automatically renew annual subscriptions or licenses online with a credit card. Choose Manual Renewal. Every vendor wants your money. They'll send an email notice before renewal is up. Pay then. Credit card companies have fraud detection, you can dispute transactions, and if valid, they arrange reimbursement.

AMEX is great in my opinion, and they are all improving because they want you to access their services much more frequently online.

Companies and institutions push online only. This is the tsunami of commerce and ecommerce in 2023. Fertile ground for criminals.

Companies and government have moved or are moving to online only transactions. Pity the poor seniors over 65 without computer skills. No more paper statements in the mail started years ago. Print it on your own printer if you want one! Nice for them because it saves the bank/company a ton of money in processing and mailing costs. **Use digital for your business.**

Keep your house in order

It's upsetting when we realize our PC, cellphone, network, etc. is compromised or corrupted. Like Chicken Little we cry, "The sky is falling!" If it's a software issue? We are out of our league. If internet solution searches or queries fail, we're stuck. Have a Chromebook, iPad, or cellphone handy to talk with the tech rep while trying to fix a main problem.

Think of your computing device, PC, laptop, or phone, as you would your house or apartment.

Your PC/ laptop is an enormous mansion, with thousands of functional rooms. Multiple systems run the heating, A/C, plumbing, electric, water, lighting, sewer, etc. Every Windows PC mansion has a Safe Room, it's brain—the Operating System (OS), on the C drive. Apple has its iOS.

The OS directs and controls the sub-systems and your libraries: Downloads for Programs; Documents; Pictures; Music; Videos; and Settings, Drivers, Registries, Indexes etc. The OS is like Alexa, Google Assistant, or Apple HomeKit

When things get messed up, it could be mundane, or extremely dangerous. It's easy for crooks to sneak into a room or file. Only if we're familiar with these rooms, what's in them, and how they normally look, feel, and function, will we notice discrepancies. **So be proactive. Pay attention.**

Get to know the right Settings.

Use utility programs

R

Software utility programs have saved my hide dozens of times. Running them gives my PC a refreshing rain shower after a full day's work in the hot fields of words, spreadsheets, and internet searches. Utility programs clean out garbage like internet trackers, temporary, junk files, and defunct or corrupt Registry entries, and more. **It amounts to gigabytes of junk.**

There are cleanup and tune-up products, like AVG's. Glary Utilities has cleaners, a software updater, an uninstaller, and many more. It's trustworthy, versatile, stable, and free.

Advanced System Care (ASC), has extensive functions too, a toolbox of quick fixes, and a RAM cleaner. Fortect is good. Pro or Premium editions of any software cost and do more.

Major software companies and anti-virus firms like Norton and McAfee are resource hogs though, and they also have Utilities which run automatically or manually, with very little info on what they're doing or did. A few specific types are:
- Driver updates like IObit's Driver Booster or Norton's
- Deleted file recovery like Recuva or EaseUS
- Disk management like Macrium Reflect
- CCleaner V.534 or higher
- File backup products, free, or fee-based like iDrive or Carbonite.

You need a utility because computers are megabyte hogs, clog up disk space and RAM, and slow your response times.

They save everything three and four ways. When Google Chrome or Edge run, they use hundreds of megabytes each even though only one window is open. Or none. Sixteen GB RAM on your device is a minimum, or paging may be slow; 32 GB RAM is better for handling bigger chunks of cache data.

Three absolute must haves are:
- **anti-virus, anti-malware software**
- **a tune-up/cleaner utility**
- **a safe search extension for browsers**

Check your browser

C*hester says: **Cybercriminals feed fake/nasty web links or code via searches. False results jump you to a malware site. Close browser tabs when not active.***

Your device connects onto the internet via Ethernet or Wi-Fi. Your business relies on a networked browser to provide internet access. **Make it your business to optimize them. It's your life's vein.** Whether Chrome, Edge/Bing, Opera, Safari, Firefox, or DuckDuckGo, tighten up Security options in their Settings.

Virtual Private Networks (VPN) are more secure. A VPN is a dedicated server and a unique IP address, so it's harder to locate you. More antivirus software products include a VPN, like

Norton 360 Deluxe. Standalone NordVPN is one of the best. However, at times you must turn a VPN off for an application to access your computer. Or turn off an adblocker to open a valid link.

If your browser is corrupted anything shown could be false.

Use a full function antivirus product with web browser or surfing safeguards added as Extensions. Some offer a green checkmark or symbol on queried links to signify "Safe."

Sources rate differently, but here's a Top 10 according to ZDNet: https://www.zdnet.com/article/best-browser-for-privacy/ Only click clean links that contain plain language, no out-of-place characters, or misspellings, and shows exactly what it is you'd expect in the URL.

The "s" in https means data is encrypted by 128-keys or more. Read the URL carefully. No typos! You have a program or certificate to authenticate data and decrypt it so that only you can read or see it. **With that, the file cannot be added to or subtracted from while in transit, a big protection.**

Don't open "http" links <u>without</u> the "s" but cybercriminals have corrupted the https standard.

They've corrupted RAM too. [X] out of the slightest weird screen or result. To test the URL to see if it's safe, copy the link (but don't open it), and paste it into Zulu's link tester at https://zulu.zscaler.com/ **Think twice before clicking an unsolicited link in any kind of message or text.**

Opening a malware link via a corrupt browser, means a click, or false email let's in a virus, malware, adware, worm, bug, trojan horse, PUP, spyware, ransomware, bot, or bad rootkit.

Hover over the blue link search result with your cursor. Look down and left. Check the actual URL at the bottom left-hand corner of your screen in the grey box.

Don't be embarrassed if you've been burned. It will happen to everyone unless world players group together and do something now. If your system is compromised, a complete restore of the Windows Operating System from a backup USB or a Windows Reset or Advanced Restore is required. Then you must reload your application programs too.

Only after a full system reset or installation can a download of your preferred browser be safe and successful.

There is only one way to be sure of a link: Type in the accurate full URL yourself in the URL field up top.

You are constantly being "tapped on the shoulder" by known or unknown trackers. Most are would-be advertisers. Microsoft tracks, Google tracks, FB, they all do. <u>Go into Privacy Settings and don't send them data anymore.</u> Use things like Ghostery.com or anti-track programs, like Norton's.

Vendors should give us a discount if they want our information for "improvement purposes," feedback, or to find out what we like. After all, it helps them earn more $$ from advertising.

Be wary of clicking long alphanumeric site addresses. Anything coming after .com/ should be logical. Search strings however can be a jumbled mix.

Don't run two or more virus programs or protective browser extensions or background utility programs simultaneously. They will clog RAM, system, memory usage, performance, and the internet. Windows Defender is always there. Your specific Virus and Threat Protection Software product overrides it.

When your browser is corrupt

Chrome, with 3.2 billion users, is the most hacked.
<u>**If your browser is corrupted, downloading a replacement program will only infect your device worse.**</u> If a hacker/criminal has installed a browser image with their instructions and replaced your good version, it's trouble. It could look like your usual browser pages. Trouble signs are:
1. Top browser search results are <u>not</u> big names or names you've seen or heard before; or weird/funky; or top names only appear on page 3, or never
2. The URL has misspellings, extra letters, or weird symbols
3. Check "About" for your browser version. It should be the latest. If it doesn't update, or fails to, it's a problem

However, out of the box, your PC with OEM hardware and software, and Microsoft Windows and its browser EDGE/Bing, should be 100% okay. When new, computers and software are designed to function without errors, without glitches, without screen flashes, warnings, or pop-ups. Computer HW & SW designers want it to work seamlessly.

That's how it should work. But viruses, malware, <u>and our own mistakes</u> enter our machines because we let them in. **<u>We ourselves are one primary source of corruptions to our machines, programs, documents, and networks.</u>** Microsoft, anti-virus companies, and all the others have no control of what we do on our own PC that creates trouble.

Tread carefully.

You'd be luckier than an excited child celebrating a 5-year birthday party with a magician, clown, and pony rides combined if you never get infiltrated or your identity stolen. Robert Downey Jr., spokesperson for Aura, said 1 in 4 of us do.

Chapter 30 Computer gotchas and fixes

C hester says: ***Commerce and eCommerce depend on computing, software, and networking systems and processes. No one is safe from disruption.***

Our human brain and our ancient animal heritage has trained our thoughts and minds, bodies, and feelings, to:
- Look for threats or try to remove them
- Flee from threats or fight them off
- Freeze up and hope for the best

We notice everything whether paying attention or not—any threat or change in our environment—no matter how tiny. Consciously or unconsciously we are in constant react mode: do something about it or ignore it.

Unless we're oblivious, which is the biggest danger. If you are oblivious on your PC/internet, you will get hurt.

In business, most think that competition is the biggest threat. In reality, the biggest threat is when we don't learn, adapt, pivot, or transition. No one can fix a problem they are unable to see or understand. "De Nile ain't just a river in Egypt." On any device, our eyes are our first line of defense. Pay attention to anomalies and address them early.

And pause before your fingers tap automatically.

Phishing attacks

What "they" don't know about you they will try to find out.

R

The government isn't your enemy, cybercriminals are. You know the term phishing. Everyone warns to be on the

lookout. But we fall for scams or false deals by the millions. **You are the reason why, not your computing device or phone.** We are suckers for what looks or feels "kosher," or piques our interest. P.T. Barnum knew it as do all con men or women who want easy $$. Gullible customers give it to them.

The internet is criminal and hacker heaven. Clicking a link, saying "Yes" on a phone call, or calling back a voicemail message number, are tried and true ways to get burnt. These modern cons play the odds: keep baiting the hook, and a fish will bite. They send out thousands of hooks at a time.

For example, I signed up online for a free Dun & Bradstreet account. Just 3 days after being accepted, I opened a voicemail from a D&B representative saying he needed to confirm the account. It gave his name and an 800 number. "Okay," I thought, "I'll call him tomorrow." By chance I looked closer.

The text of the voicemail said, "Dunning and Bradstreet."

A real agent would not have said "Dunning." This caller knew I had signed up for Dun & Bradstreet. I didn't do it by phone, but through my Chrome browser. However, he also had my cellphone number, a double whammy.

Bottom line: our identifying information, name, address, phone #, SS#, is plastered in records everywhere, public and private. This "agent" got it from D&B (doubtful), from my Chrome browser, bought it for a buck, or picked through my recycle bucket out at the curb one morning.

That's exactly what cookies and trackers do. Those constant "nudges on your shoulder," or signing up for things, buying things, searches on the net, all provide intel about you.

Lessons learned:
- Shred mail, paper, bills etc. with identifying info on it
- Use Anti-Tracker software like Ghostery, Norton or others
- Use protective browser extensions and settings
- Don't be careless when sharing data
- Think twice before responding to an unsolicited call
- **Look twice, stop, read carefully, and think again.**

Note too, hackers may just want to destroy things for fun. Criminals want to trick you or ransom you for $$.

Save your bacon

R

Most of us aren't tech gurus. Heck, we'd like to trust computers, they can work great. We all need them. But they, and we, make mistakes. Why this security and tech jargon?

In this age of the holy Trinity of computer hardware, software, and networking were prisoners of, there are seriously bad actors. If you can save your files from their malware, corruption, and thievery, make your devices safe, optimize your systems, or unclog your storage, you'll be happier. Here are a few tips to ensure that:

#1 Use Encryption

Since 2001 with the AES standard, data uses 128, 192, or 256-key encryption methods. Bitlocker is a better one, but Microsoft doesn't think we home users should have it. Tsk tsk.

#2 Run a periodic version image scan on Windows

Every morning take a minute to ensure your Windows Operating System is secure. In Glary Utilities, click "Repair System Files" or at the command prompt, run **sfc /scannow** as the administrator.

If it completes and says, "Resource Protection did not find any integrity violations," you're good to go. IF NOT, if it repaired a corruption, type the three DISM commands, checkhealth, scanhealth, restorehealth. Answers.microsoft.com has the format. It takes six minutes. "Exit" when done.

#3 Windows tech help

If your computer acts weird and built-in Windows Troubleshooters can't fix it, click any blue "Get Help" link in Settings. Follow the prompts and be taken to a live MS technician, 24/7. Give them your information and Windows version, like 22H2 or 23H2. They will never ask for a credit card. Repairs go quicker if you're tech savvy.

<u>Be specific and describe issues in the Chat</u>. **Be patient. Be nice. <u>Write down the case number.</u>** Let them diagnose the issue remotely through Quick Assist. Ask questions. Take notes. MAKE SURE THE ISSUE IS FIXED BEFORE ENDING CHAT. Complete the survey.

#4 Backup your Documents, Pictures, and files

Since 2007, with the release of Windows OneDrive, backing up Documents, Pictures, Music, and Videos takes place automatically in the cloud. Word docs aren't automatically saved to your hard drive unless you specify "Keep a copy on my computer." OneDrive is synced if you see a grey cloud icon in the lower right taskbar, or a blue one for an organization.

If no icon, type "app: onedrive" in the search box and "enter." It will appear and sync. Google does similarly with Drive.

Backing up your data files is an investment that saves time, aggravation, and money.

An external 1TB drive attached by USB copies files locally or save your data into another cloud storage backup resource like Carbonite.com. It costs extra but is a business expense and an investment. A cheaper way is to buy a Flash Drive and copy certain files or keep biz records in a safe deposit box.

#5 Make sure File History runs

Windows File History is Microsoft's way to keep your data safe, with snapshots by date and time. If problems, go to "Control Panel" and restore from an untainted copy.

#6 Know your Programs

Programs and Applications on your computer are kept in the Downloads Folder but only for setup. Programs themselves reside in Program Folders on your C: drive. If you lose your PC, you'll have to download and reload your Programs from scratch, possibly via Login to your accounts from vendor sites.

If your PC crashes, you must reload all Programs from scratch. That's your job.

When you buy/download an app or program, keep a record of the vendor's website, the application, your Login ID, Password, your email account address, <u>and the alphanumeric license or product activation code.</u>

Always print out and save vendor invoices or payment receipts, especially with a license/activation code on it. **Vendors today, even government, communicate by email, not by mail. Save those emails. Print and file them.**

7 Create a USB recovery drive

Whatever Operating System you run, make a recovery drive using Settings. If your system crashes, you'll be able to restore your last good version and your settings. Have two 16GB flash drives and write over the earliest one.

#8 Clean your Registry

The Registry contains critical but often temporary information that Windows uses during operations. Almost everything passes through Registry keys. Many of its entries are created by running programs or tasks which are invalid when over. Some folks say, "It doesn't need to be cleaned that much." Hogwash. Use a Utility Program to clean it regularly.

Hackers love to corrupt it and make evil registry keys. A corrupt Registry or Rootkit can prevent your computer from running, restarting, shutting down, or booting.

One fault with every computer is that they do not clean out garbage well automatically. **Computers are space hogs. Duplication runs rampant.** Clean it up, like closing still open apps on your iPhone with swipes of your finger.

#9 Become a mini-tech guru

Your business PC and the Internet are critical. Learn how to recognize and solve problems. Use technology to fix specifics, even get daily tips from iPhone Life for your iPhone. Subscribe free to Tech Guru and author Bob Rankin's daily emails on everything related to pcs, viruses, malware, Windows, backups, networks, internet, applications, Wi-Fi, smartphones and more. For his go to https://askbobrankin.com

Check Ask your Computer Guy or MDTech on YouTube, Tech Republic.com, CNET, ZDNet or PCMag. **There's a great resource list at https://www.techrepublic.com/resource-library/**

#10 Use your vendor, you paid for it

Warranty or fee-based help is available from your hardware or software vendor, or online at techsolutions, microcenter.com, asktech.support, or justanswer.com. Best Buy's Geek Squad and Staples Tech Centers are in their stores for carry-in device repairs and virus removal.

Ad blockers

Pesky, pesky, pesky ads! In your browsed webpages, searches, online documents like blogs and articles, YouTube, FB, Amazon et al. An ad blocker extension helps, software that keeps the ad from showing or popping up. AdBlock, Total Adblock, Ghostery, or AdBlock Plus are a few of dozens.

Unclog storage

The most critical drive you have on your PC device is the C: drive. It stores all Windows system files, settings, registry, everything. If you clog it with Documents, Pictures, Music et al., it will fill up and you'll have problems.

In Windows Settings, under System, click Storage and see your drives' storage usage and clean out old files and junk. You can recover files with Recuva if make a mistake.

Utilities keep your machine fast and sleek.

Chapter 31 "I've been robbed!"

*C**hester Says:* **Don't be complacent. Robbed of $$ is one thing. Don't be robbed of your good reputation.**

Beside you and your things, valuables are:
- Your home and place of business
- Your electronic and communication devices and access
- Your $$, bank account, and other financial accounts
- Your business records and files
- Your identity or your reputation

Family and friends are valuable too, and those you rely upon. Take care of them and be mindful you don't lose or hurt them through carelessness.

Secure your possessions

G

What we had not done at our first learning center, we did at our new place. Install a locking door security system.

We hadn't thought of buying one until someone stopped by the office and convinced us of the wisdom of protecting all our equipment and furnishings.

It made good sense, and we were no longer close to a police station as we had been. A vendor installed it, and Ilene and I made it a habit to deactivate the system as soon as we entered the building. Only once did we have to call the company to reset it.

We felt secure with it in place.

One late morning as I was tutored a student in a cubicle, I noticed a man pass by whom I had not seen before. I walked to the front of the office and asked Ilene, who was talking to a woman across from her desk, who he was. Her reply was that he had asked to use the restroom.

I returned to tutoring, but after several minutes wondered why the man was taking so long, so I walked to the end of the corridor leading to the bathroom just as he was exiting it.

I stood directly in front of him and said something like, "How's it going?" He replied that the woman at the front of our office had said it was okay for him to use the bathroom. He then went to the front of the office and left with the woman with whom Ilene had been speaking.

Less than an hour later, Ilene ordered lunch from the restaurant next door, so she lifted her purse from the floor of the inner office and looked inside for the small wallet she kept within it—it was missing.

She yelled, startling me, "I've been robbed!"

The wallet had $230 in it but fortunately, contained no credit cards.

The woman had purposely distracted Ilene, asking inane questions about the brochures that had been left by various businesses on a shelf near the front desk, to allow her accomplice to take a few seconds to reach around the corner of a doorway to our inner office, open Ilene's purse and withdraw her wallet.

We immediately called the police and were told we could go to the central station three miles away and file a report.

We drove there, careful not to describe to each other descriptions of the two people who had come in simultaneously, for we did not want to influence each other's recollections.

Ilene spoke first to an officer while I waited in the parking lot; then I spoke to him.

Remarkably, our descriptions were similar, although Ilene knew more about the woman, and I more about the man.

He was in his thirties, six feet tall with close-cropped hair, an athletic build, and violet eyes. The woman was in her forties, five feet three inches, with blonde hair and glasses.

When I described the man, the officer stated he had a good idea who it was—especially with my description of the suspect's violet eyes—for he lived in a half-way house less than a mile from our office. The office gave me a case number, a detective's name, and a telephone number.

Back at work, Ilene and I did a little detective work of our own. We found that a person in the jewelry store next door had eyed the same man, who had stood in front of the store next to his dark, late-model sedan talking to someone on his cellular phone. I also spoke to the manager of the bank across from the street, hoping the camera of his drive-up window caught the man's license plates, but it didn't have that long a range.

A few weeks later, we learned that the same woman entered the Brandermill community office and tried to walk back into the inner portion of the office, but the person there stopped her.

We were told to call 9-1-1 if either of the suspects showed up again, but they never did. We purchased a security camera and set up an alarm system, but after a few months, we seldom set the alarm. The camera, however, conveniently enabled us to see who was entering the office if we were in the back room. We also installed a motion detector that rang a bell in the back of the office in case we were not within view of the front door.

Always report a crime. Cooperate with police.

Wallets, cash, and credit cards are harder to steal when they are on one's person, although we all know about pickpockets in crowds who work in teams, like the movie *Focus.* **Staff in an office or store environment need a lockable file drawer, locker, or cabinet to house things such as purses.**

R

I received an inquiry from a man on LinkedIn. We exchanged thoughts online, and he said he was Baha'i too. He had an academic paper he wanted edited and I said, "Be happy too." I sent him a one-page agreement. He sent me his paper. I started on it, expecting the agreement back soon. I didn't ask him for advance payment; the amount was small.

After two days, I emailed him. No response. I checked his LinkedIn profile—gone. Emailed him again—returned undeliverable. I had been scammed. He was phishing.

Luckily, I run virus scans daily. If there had been one in his paper, it would have been caught. I was doubly lucky.

Lessons learned: Get paid before starting a job, and do not provide much personal identifying information. Keep it all business.

Thieves want your identity details to get to your $$. They get in because you let them in, or they get, steal, even buy your information from the Dark Web.

Chapter 32 Politics and policies

Chester says: ***Your beliefs may conflict with those of your customers or potential clients. Remain neutral.***

Religion and politics are integral to every aspect of birth, life, work, society, and death. Humans accomplish great things through cooperation when unified, or the worst when misguided or disunited. Human behavior knows no bounds unless moderation, consultation, and common sense guide them.

Politics, laws, regulations, social norms, and cultural forces affect your business. Stay abreast of what's current.

Stay neutral in controversies if possible. Having good policies provides a safe haven for what may occur.

G

Inquiries about tutoring at the Learning Center often came from students' mothers. The first question was whether we tutored a particular subject, the next, "What hours are you open?" followed by, "How much do lessons cost?"

Occasionally, a couple would enter, and on rare occasions, a grandparent. Once, a school age boy did.

Clients may be different than the decision maker who buys or pays for your services. Cater to both.
Think married couples and parents for example.

Adults wishing their child to prepare for standardized testing, or improve their reading, or learn English, formed the kind of clients we served.

Half the parents remained in our learning center waiting room as we tutored their children; others enjoyed visiting with Ilene. **She realized the importance of good public relations,** but eventually longed to have more time for herself. Not goofing off, but rather paying bills, making copies of materials, writing blogs for our website, and receiving and making phone calls. Those were difficult while chatting with others.

This resulted in her moving permanently into our inner office and abandoning the front desk we had purchased for welcoming people.

Those who greet and direct visitors should have other work to do.

Most parents who came to us focused on the effectiveness of the lessons, but some made their religious and political views known. This was to test us, and it was difficult not to respond negatively.

One set of parents had moved from Oak Ridge, New Jersey, where my first wife and I had lived. Their children had attended the same middle school as my two children had. The excitement over this coincidence ended abruptly when the father stated, "President Obama is a Muslim and wants a new world order that will eliminate our country's freedoms." Confusion aside, we did not want to argue facts.

Many Christians came to our center, and one posted online that "Chesterfield Learning Center is run by two wonderful

Christians." Ilene and I debated whether to reveal that Ilene was Jewish. When she finally did, the mother accepted it, saying, "Oh, you are the chosen people." I seldom, if ever, revealed my religious preferences other than saying, "I occasionally attend services at a Unitarian Universalist Fellowship."

Be wary of assumptions. In 2022, 64% of American adults were Christians. It used to be 90% in 1972. Views and beliefs change. (Source Pew Research)

Over the years, several parents appreciated our tutoring with gifts—mainly during Christmas. One couple bought us a huge plant and also gave a few pounds of grapes the size of golf balls. This mother often asked Ilene to join her shopping. Some parents gave gift cards, either general ones or such as Western Sizzler or Bonefish Grill. One parent even gave us a stack of two-dollar bills. It flattered us they cared and said much about the quality of our services.

Websites are "On" 24 hours a day. Check regularly for any messages or contacts made to your business email address. They'll occur while you sleep!

Seldom did we have complaints, but a few parents took advantage. One mother paid for two daughters to learn Chinese, but then asked if her third daughter could simply "sit in and listen." Of course, the tutor, whom we were paying extra to teach two children at once, could not ignore the child.

That same parent, who was home schooling her children, asked us to give one of them a grade level achievement test.

Not all people are reasonable. Offer a partial refund but get paid for what you've done.

When we did and reported that she was seriously behind in her learning, the mother became upset and chided us! She said, "I did not pay you to inform me my child is not meeting recommended standards." We refunded her money. We were not about to lie just because she had paid us.

One mother tried our patience several times, but we were nevertheless pleased to help her son. She would occasionally call and ask for a tutor the next day, or even the same evening.

Once she called while Ilene and I were at my son's wedding and Ilene made the mistake of answering. The mom expressed great disappointment that we were not available to help her son prepare for a test on Monday.

Most parents became acquaintances or friends because we were a face-to-face business. Ilene made them feel comfortable by genuinely inquiring about their weekends, their children, and their jobs. Such interactions made the overall business more enjoyable than it could otherwise be.

People differ. They don't view things the same, they don't react the same. Treat them with courtesy, respect, and honesty, but stick to reasonable principals.

Another assumption of ours was that a public nonprofit business organization would be neutral in its politics.

At one meeting I attended, a Republican delegate was a guest speaker and ended his speech by denigrating President Obama. Everyone gave him a standing ovation—except for a woman at my table and me. Others at the table looked at us with disdain, but at least I got to know her and her husband, and Ilene and I had dinner at their home soon after.

After attending a few meetings with a different organization, Ilene officially joined. The stated goals of the group were noble, but we soon realized several members appeared to be racist, or at least ultra conservative, so Ilene ceased attending.

The customer

Chester says: *The customer is not always right—until they are.*

R

Everyone is human. We make mistakes. We misinterpret. We don't know all the facts. We jump to wrong conclusions. We have feelings and emotions that get stirred up. We can't read minds. If we perceive we've been treated unfairly we get angry. Or we're having a bad day.

You are in the middle of the customer and your business. You are advocate and supporter of both—and a few sour customers can be nightmares. Positive customer reviews jumpstart any business. Negative ones or complaints harm reputations, brands, and sales.

The solution? Be nice. Be polite and fair. Have and post fair policies. Be able to defend your actions or nonactions. Some companies have a Customer Bill of Rights, like the Federal Consumer Bill of Rights of eight points. Be quick to show you are an upstanding citizen.

> *Facts and evidence are solid defenses.*
> *Emotional words and actions are not.*

My mother needed a new queen mattress. We looked at ads in the newspaper and Sleepy's stood out for $399 and it was a name brand. We drove over. We walked the floor and didn't see it. I asked the sales agent to see the one advertised.

He took us to a dingy corner and pulled out an ugly, small-sized uncovered mattress. It reminded me of those I'd had when age 17 in Juvenile Hall and County Jail.

He said, "Here it is. But you should look at others."

His duplicity appalled and stunned me. The ad was false, made solely to get us into the store and upsell us. I wanted to call the police, but Mom said no. We left. I hope they've changed their tactics now that they're part of Mattress Firm.

Don't lie, act illegally, or cruelly. Don't be disrespectful or duplicitous. **Be courteous and honest. Introduce yourself and call others by name. Be flexible, yet firm in principle.** Post your policies. Courtesy is the Prince of all virtues.

You as owner

You own your business, but you can't do everything you'd wish to or like to. There are major constraints, such as:
- income or staffing
- following government rules and regulations
- hours available in the day
- personal vs. business commitments
- surprises, always surprises

There are major freedoms too:
- flexible hours
- ability to change prices higher or lower
- ability to postpone or reschedule
- make rules or policies or change them
- ability to hire or fire
- ability to negotiate

Freedom with restraint. The opposite is anarchy and chaos like the January 6th attack on the U.S. Capitol.

You are the President, Queen, Principal, or King of your own business. Your face is the face of your kingdom and empire. How you act and speak, even dress, is how your business acts. **You set the goals, do the work, direct the work, and make rules. Manage and guide it well and it reflects well on you.**

> "You don't build a business, you build the people, then people build the business."—Zig Ziglar

Business, like life, is maintaining a good balance between personal demands, working, and trying to reach your business goals.

Assume nothing

The word "assume," when broken down, is "ass u me." "Assumptions make an ass out of you and me…."
Assumptions equal poor decisions and horrid communications.

The phrase "assume nothing" is good to follow. But do not assume the worst about people or situations. Let things play out and decide then unless you absolutely must intervene. People aren't idiots, but sometimes do stupid things. You can hate the idiotic thing they did, but not them, not the whole person. We all have good qualities and a few bad. Separate individual behaviors or actions from the whole person.

Keep that uppermost because you will deal with hundreds or thousands of people. Many will think or feel they are right and you are wrong. **Don't ever talk or write in anger or haste. Check your speech and flying fingertips at the door.**

G

We made a few poor assumptions in our business transactions that taught us valuable lessons.

We had been tutoring the daughter of a couple for several months just before we informed them, we were moving. When we mentioned we would have to repaint the entire new place, the father remarked he would help us. He had supplies too, including a sander, paint brushes, rollers, and even a ladder.

We agreed we could barter tutoring for painting. However, we failed to mention whether an hour of painting equaled an hour of tutoring. As a means of comparison, an air conditioning serviceman cost $120 per hour, whereas our average tutoring fee was $45 per hour.

Regardless, Ilene and I decided the barter would be an even swap, hour for hour. The man was a pleasure to work with as Ilene and I painted with him side-by-side. The first few weeks he came in a few hours every other day, but after a month, we seldom saw him. When the new learning center was open, we called him in with his wife and discussed how much money they owed us for tutoring their daughter.

The sum added up to hundreds of dollars.

However, unbeknown to us, the father had not informed his wife that he had stopped helping us, and she assumed he painted the entire inside of the new center, but it was only a fourth.

We ended up asking for much less than we were owed and were quite disappointed that communication between the parents had not been better. The daughter took no more lessons from us.

Assumptions come from poor communications. **Clarify/Verify.** *Get it in writing, especially where $$, time, and expectations are concerned.*

We were having problems with students cancelling sessions. At the end of six months, Ilene and I added an important notice to the bottom of our student questionnaire. This was to help prevent us having to pay a tutor when a student did not show up as planned. In bold it said, **"48 hours' notice needed for any changes in the schedule"**.

However, within two years we encountered enough problems with schedules to force us to make another change. A few parents had insisted that they had **not** agreed upon a particular day and hour for tutoring, even though they had.

From then on, when printing out a schedule of tutoring for the parents' benefit, we made two copies: one for them (or student) and one for us. Each parent(s) had to initial our copy of the schedule. To be diplomatic, I'd say, "This will ensure the schedule is accurate," and initial the parent's/student's copy. I asked them to reciprocate, "So I know you have received a copy."

We never again had a parent challenge us on what the schedule had been.

Reduce your terms to writing in clear English and obtain written consent. Post signs and policies.

Part Four Grow

You should be settled in. You've absorbed a lot of information, sorted through it, established routines, made lists and goals, set your priorities, and have marching plans. You need and want consistent growth. You want to foster a good reputation and wide recognition in the marketplace. You want to use available tools and resources to move sales.

Here's the nitty-gritty on How.

Chapter 33 Better opportunities

Chester says: ***When you find an ideal location, move there quickly. Online too. Take immediate advantage of opportunities.***

G

A dance studio occupied two units in our strip mall. We noticed it was expanding to the unit abutting ours—and sensed trouble. I entered the studio and spoke to those setting up.

Gently, I informed them our tutoring business required a quiet environment. I said, "We hope any music or noise from the new space will be kept low, or at least classical, rather than the hip hop and rap music I often heard coming from this place."

Within a couple of weeks, however, our worse fears came true: loud thumping music blasted through the wall. I was livid and went next door and addressed the person instructor. I informed her we were legally entitled to a quiet environment, and that she must turn down the volume. She did.

The next day, the owner, which catered to several hundred students, came to our office, and stated I had scared the instructor the night before. I explained our need for quiet and shortly thereafter called the leasing company.

An agent came out and spoke to the dance studio owner and us. We explored solutions. This included placing their music speakers on stands facing away from our common wall. However, this had little effect.

Circumstances can be out of your control.
We can get mad, sick, pout, endure them,
or do something about it.

We had an attorney examine our leasing contract, only to explain that the term "quiet" in leases had nothing to do with noise! Rather, it addressed the fact that landlords cannot enter lessees' premises without permission or just cause. We were fighting a losing battle, so had to schedule students around the dance studio's times of operation.

Despite knowing what upheavals and cost it would entail, the starting over, setting up, opening, and resuming, we decided to move. We began looking in the fall of 2013.

Since our landlord had issued us a strictly enforced lease, we needed to provide a notice of intent to vacate at least six months before the three-year lease ended; otherwise, we could be indebted to the company for another three years.

Your workplace must be conducive to getting
things done, not distracting.

Since the loud music from the dance studio next door was disruptive when tutoring, we had no choice but move. Where?

Following up on a lead by a Facebook acquaintance of Ilene's, I drove three miles east of our learning center to an area called Market Square.

The move turns superior

G

The best word to describe Market Square was *quaint*. Area businesses formed a square missing one side. It occupied four acres of land and was at the juncture of three busy highways, one of them an entrance to Brandermill, a huge development covering many square miles.

The place I heard about was the last vacant one in the Square, amid heavily trafficked stores like a jeweler's, food market, pub, post office and more. If we wanted to secure it for our learning center, we would have to do so quickly. I drove to it and looked through its windows.

I was impressed at once, for beyond its large foyer stood a wall with an opening about six feet wide, leading to another large, dark area. On either side were fluted columns and there were also niches just begging for vases or busts.

My immediate reaction through the dim light was that this place had once had class. Within a week, Ilene and I were inside with a realtor and the leasing agent. We found nearly all the floors in deplorable shape, and the inner office was plain weird, but we felt we could renovate.

We were given the option of adding our learning center name to that of other businesses on a tall tower alongside busy Hull Street Road. We realized that as we drove past; it was impossible to read all the names unless stopped in traffic. **For once, we resisted one more opportunity to "get our name out there" and saved several hundred dollars.**

Our homework told us the nearby development of Brandermill was 2,444 acres, with 3,700 homes. If just one percent of those homes needed tutoring for a child, 37 children coming in twice a week would meet our expenses, netting $6,000 per month.

We signed the three-year lease, having been granted three months' free rent. We set about renovating.

Within four months, we were in business again. **Nearly all our former clients remained with us, and because of more foot traffic from the popular Italian restaurant and other Town Square stores, we rapidly increased our client base.**

Never sign an agreement without a cancellation clause. It can be a life saver.

However, for six months we had to pay rent both for the original and the new locations. Ilene traveled to the previous site on the rare occasions that we had a student or two meet with one of our tutors there.

By the end of the year, we had more than made up for the difference. Truly, location is paramount when establishing or re-establishing a walk-in business. In this case, although the move wasn't meant as an expansion, it worked out as one monetarily and we benefited with increased income.

For any business, online or walk-in, profile the number of potential customers. Set targets and goals every month.

By the end of our sixth year as the new Chesterfield Learning Center, we were tutoring seventy students per week. We also frequently used an area in the center's rear for paint parties, sewing lessons and occasional tutoring of more than one student for preparation for the PRAXIS exam, for entrance into teaching programs. We were ecstatic about the revenue, readily met expenses, and had money for our salaries.

Business of the Month

G

The manager of a bank branch with which we did business was our store neighbor. We had noticed that the bank each month sponsored a Small Business of the Month. We discussed having a small display in his foyer. He was pleased to accommodate us.

We set it up as we had done with so many other attempts to advertise, hoping that people would see it, read one of our Chesterfield Learning Center brochures on the table, and sign up for tutoring. As usual, we found no evidence that it brought us any business. But we hoped someone might tell anyone who needed tutoring something like, "Oh, your child needs some tutoring? I saw a display at the bank and picked this up."

You never know when your ads, words, displays, current customers, even strangers will mention you to others. But only results prove the case. ***Always measure results.***

We agreed that static displays, as much as they may catch someone's eye, were not enough to generate business. From the many booths we had manned, it was obvious that unless passersby sought tutoring, we were simply ignored.

**A shotgun is not as accurate as a rifle with a mounted scope. Both however serve a distinct purpose when hunting.
Promote and market to your audience. Be where it is.**

Chapter 34 Do better than breakeven

Chester says: ***Successful advertising results in enough sales to pay for and exceed the costs of ads.***

B A L A N C E is more than a 7-letter word

Balance at its heart is moderation in all things. Our speech, actions, ads we push, sales pitches, etc. all seek to exert influence on another. But when carried to excess cause evil, hurt, pain, and disgust.

Business is sales, sales is business, the foundation of commerce. As owners its always asking someone the question, "What can I do to make you willing to spend your money?" And we must spend our own money too, to accommodate others needs, wants, and desires. We do that well and we'll grow, a simple life equation.

R

There's a universal breakeven formula for deciding whether to go forward with a project. It doesn't matter one bit if its widgets, services, or rocket parts. I learned it in 1983 while working for the State. It means the actual cost is paid for by units sold, hence, breakeven. **To make a profit, units must be sold, or income made, beyond the breakeven point.**

Formula: **Units sold minus cost of units equals result**
Or ask, "How many units do I need to sell to cover my cost?"
Formula: **Project cost minus (Unit cost x number sold)**

Always calculate the breakeven point. The goal is to profit from your expenditure, not throw $$ away. You need a positive Return on Investment (ROI).

Don't forget for one minute, that total cost means TOTAL. You must get a handle on expenses by project, task, or activity. Get in the habit of applying the formula for Breakeven and Payback Analysis to your expenditures. This is triply important if you make your living from your business.

Like in a restaurant, you should know what ingredients cost, staffing, and overhead to calculate meal prices, volume you project to sell, and what market prices are.

*The simplest breakeven formula to remember is **Income less Expenses equals Balance.***

Say I have an ad campaign/budget on Facebook that costs $100/day for 6 days for impressions clicked, that's $600 for my project cost. If that campaign is to drive customers to Amazon to buy my books at an average profit in royalties paid to me of $5/book, I'd have to sell 120 books to breakeven.

As we've said, a decent profit is 20%. I'd have to sell 144 books, 24 more, to reach the goal of 120%.

Or say I sell my editing services to writers at $40/hour. The campaign, or ad, or software I'm buying, or rent/electricity/utilities/software I'm paying or whatever, totals $800/month. I'd have to do editing work for 20 hours to breakeven. Plus 20% more for profit, or $160, equal to 4 more hours.

See where this is going? **Do it for what you sell.**

Monitor Income and Expenses or wind up in red ink.

Also keep the whole business and your life picture in perspective. They are intertwined. Breakeven and payback analysis are critical strategies to move ahead with projects, whether personal or business. Business owners must monitor income, sales, and profits from every source, less expenses.

This is Cash Flow. It rarely equals 1:1. Don't be alarmed; be aware. Some projects or days breakeven, others make more or less. That's normal.

Greenlight projects, ad campaigns etc. based on specific goals, objectives and surpassing breakeven.

Reaching eyeballs or ears primarily promotes brand awareness and is one goal. It's a much tougher requirement to pass breakeven with sales and make that 20% profit. **It also costs more to sell than it does to inform.**

Paying for awareness has less payback than targeted marketing or advertising geared to generate buzz <u>and</u> make direct sales and conversions. Giveaways are like that.

First decide your goal before shelling out funds for an ad campaign. How many gadgets or how much $$$ in services must you make to surpass breakeven?

Get off the ground

Chester says: ***There are dozens of marketing methods, from direct mail, to email, to blogging, to SEO, to texting, social media, and inbound or outbound too.***

Think and act consistently across the three Integrated Marketing venues: **platforms, media, and materials**.

A consistent logo, a memorable company name, a respected brand, website, and email name, these show what you do and who you are. It's like your company phone number: you wouldn't change it. **Basics don't change but ads must. What attracts audiences change and so do marketplaces. Heck, the weather changes by minute. Fads pop like balloons. That can mean changing your products, services, and prices.**

Values change, laws change, situations and circumstances change. But you must be the Rock of Gibraltar; steady, desirable, helpful, and reliable no matter what you sell.

G

What better way to reach several hundred people than to have flyers about our learning center delivered directly to their homes?

It was cheaper than direct mail, what with buying an address list, making/printing what to send, like a postcard, the cheapest, addressing it, and postage for mailing. Then there was the bulk mail process itself that had tight USPS restrictions.

We knew it was illegal to put things in mailboxes, per Section 508.3.-1.3 of the Domestic Mail Manual. But unlike New Jersey, in our area of Virginia comprised of large subdivisions with separate cubbies below them, they were specifically designed for flyers, brochures, or the occasional note from a neighbor announcing a party.

Two different companies in our immediate area offered services for putting flyers into these cubbies, with various plans. One could choose subdivision A, for instance, and reach 650 homes, or subdivision B and reach 925 homes, or both, for a discount. We tried outreach to homes in two subdivisions within a few miles of our center. We copied several hundred flyers ourselves, and the company picked them up for delivery.

Printed copy in someone's hands is an advantage over fleeting messages on phones, radio, or social media.

Within the month we had been in business, Ilene had met three people who lived in these subdivisions, about to be inundated with our flyers. A few days after the delivery date, she called them to see what they thought.

They never received them. We were disappointed. And angry.

We called the delivery company, and they said, "Occasionally a driver skips some homes to follow the company rule: If a box already contains at least six pieces of paper, the flyer can't be delivered. Mainly because the homeowner won't look at any of them."

Use quality control. Monitor the effectiveness of your products/services, marketing, advertising, and delivery.

We were suspicious. We discussed whether it would make sense to deliver flyers ourselves. This would mean not only spending the time when we could have been doing something else, but also spending money on gas. We mapped out a route carefully to maximize delivery efficiency.

Ilene thought this would be a waste of time, but one night, around 2:00 a.m., unable to sleep, I drove to the center, collected a few hundred flyers, and entered a large subdivision.

I discovered at such an early hour I could drive on the left side of the road and insert the flyers into the neighborhood boxes out my driver-side window. What I did not realize, however, was that the turning arcs on some of the cul-de-sacs were so tight that the car's left rear wheel occasionally rubbed against the curb, or against the iron bracket that lay atop sewer grates.

I had taken Ilene's new car, because it got better gas mileage, and she was not pleased the next day when seeing scrape marks on the wheel rim.

Your time costs money. Weigh that against hiring out a service to do it. Monitor payback and benefits in direct income made.

My efforts paid off, though—to a small extent. Within a few days, we got a call from a student who had just graduated from a nearby high school and was entering an engineering school in the fall. He felt he did not know calculus as well as he should and wanted to be sure he could start strongly from the first day of class in September.

Fortunately, we had available a math tutor who could help him, and we profited by $200 for the entire summer, the cost to replace the wheel rim I had scuffed.

*The best of all worlds is when the customer calls, texts, emails, or contacts you. **This is inbound sales.***
  Have processes set up to follow up.

Refine your brand

R

Brand names identity you.
    Customers remember company names, brand names, logos, and slogans as key identifiers of what they like or want, so companies protect their use commercially. If they meet USPTO.gov criteria, some names, logos, or slogans may be trademarked. Seeing them consistently makes them memorable.
    But ideas or things like titles cannot be legally copyrighted. These tongue-in-cheek slogans below may ring a bell:

Lowes *Knows home improvement* and
Home Depot is *How doers get things done*,
like me, a homeowner, reliant on both.
    With Nike sneakers on my feet I *Just do it*
or I'm *All in or nothing* if I wear Adidas,
but I also believe the Sketchers promise,
Good for the feet. Good for the world.
    I hear Tony the tiger shout, *They're grrreat!*
when hawking Kellogg's Frosted Flakes
and saw General Mills put Batman's bat symbols
and Superman's big red S on munchkin's plates.
    Walmart replaced *Always low prices, always*
with *Save money. Live better* for when I visit,
and Best Buy wants intercourse when they say
Let's talk about what's possible.
    Companies, brands, products, logos, slogans,
from top to bottom meant to give us the urge—
select from a shelf or buy with a click,
once we've tried it, easy to come back.

(Above company names, brands, or products above may be registered or trademarked)

    If you use your name or initials in your company name, that's your major brand. It is the public face of your company and helps you stand out from the competition. Like thousands of companies do, you might sell products or service packages with special names, also called brand names, and they deserve top billing as well.

Logos and slogans bring familiarity to your company brand or a product or service brand. They focus marketing and ad campaigns, develop recognition, and bring repeat customers. **Customers are most likely to choose a brand known for credibility, trustworthiness, and value.** We know hundreds and hundreds of brands and see or hear of them over decades because companies never stop marketing. **A marketing budget is a bottom-line mandatory company expense.**

Once customers like a product or brand they return for it, like my bag of baby Mounds bars or Entenmann's Chocolate-Frosted Donuts from ACME. My sweet tooth wouldn't like it if either were no longer available. **Customers grow attached to the things they like and return to where they bought them. That means a box store or online, your website or another.**

Brainstorm and test your brand name or slogan for SEO results. Use your company name, brands, logos, and slogans profusely. Advertisements can have their own catchy phrase or slogan per ad or a campaign.

When we think of the best ads, we think Super Bowl, and they cost millions of dollars to produce and air. But that's worth it to advertisers who had 123 million viewers in 2024, followed by YouTube views. **Ads that titillate, invoke surprise or laughter, or touch our minds, hearts, or feelings, all sell products.** Even the flops are memorable, like Apple's star-studded 2023 "Grill the CEO." I liked it, some didn't. But you got the message that Apple cares for the environment.

Chapter 35 Sales and marketing goals

Chester says: *No written goals or Business and Marketing Plans? No success.*

Commerce is tough. There's always competition. You're up against seasoned, well-paid professional advertisers with deep pockets and marketers in expert high-priced firms better than any actor ad man like Jon Hamm. As well as amateurs. Millions of them. But startups succeed all the time, and big names close.

SBA.gov and SCORE.org help with any business question you'll face, including business and marketing plans, free articles, webinars and podcasts, and free personal counseling and training on Zoom, email, or phone. They offer access to sources of capital, Federal contracting, even disaster relief. SBA has 1,000 offices in 50 states and more.

They provide one-to-one in-person help on advertising and marketing. According to SCORE news, in November 2023, SCORE mentored 125,397 unique clients last year. Ninety percent of "in-business" clients stayed in business; 55% of those reported increased revenue.

Refer to and use SBA.gov and SCORE.org resources and mentors often.

---

https://BigIdeasforSmallBusiness.com has daily info, notices, and help from Barbara Welder, with short bulletins, legal tips, and more by email. Another source is the Chamber of Commerce, locally and nationally. Although expensive to join, they list some good connections.

Depend on your website host like a Squarespace or Wix and their abilities to create webpage URLs, improve SEO, and add automatic responses. Convey your services pricing with one email, text, post etc. with an included link that takes them directly to that page on your website. Use specific page links anywhere, on social media, texts, in ads, on marketing materials etc. Use a specific name, not a generic "click here," and use https:// to show its secure.

Specific pages, ads, texts etc. can be a QR code, the hottest thing to use right now, even shown on tv screens. They are also huge in the app ordering and delivery game. Use one to take someone to your webpage, ad, anywhere you like. Some can be fake, so it helps if you're a known quantity.

Just remember. It's not the ad. It's the content they get to that creates their urge to buy and seals the deal.

Set goals or fail

Many years ago, Harvard conducted a student study. They asked how many had goals. Some did, many did not. They asked how many told others their goals. Some had, some hadn't. Then they asked how many had written goals.

Some did, but fewer.

They studied this large group over many years to see if they achieved their goals. Those who verbalized them had achieved a small percentage of success. Those who had also written them down had done much better and were 10 times more successful in wealth and careers. Those who had none, well….

You must be focused, tough, and determined. Goals are the start. Do not follow your "gut," or go by the seat of your pants. Write a plan, follow the plan. Be a Michelin Chef who gets a three-star rating, meaning your restaurant, "your business," gets that too. Start with your written Business Plan. **The first rule is that goals must be specific and measurable.**

"A man, a plan, a canal, Panama," is a palindrome after for the incredible building of the Panama Canal between a false start in 1881, and real work from 1904-1914.

"You can't improve what you can't measure."—W. Edwards Deming. Measure the bang of every marketing or advertising buck spent. Give it time, but if no measurable results, profits, or customers, then dump it. If positive, continue or expand.

Objectives are the steps taken or planned to achieve the goals and should also be specific. Write down estimated and known expenses, including your salary. Some are fixed, some discretionary. Break them down by month. Add the 12 months. Add 20% profit. That's the minimum revenue you need for the year, your first goal.

Refine your Marketing Plan. A yearly calendar is a good place to start, including advertising campaigns. **Set marketing/advertising budgets, then set sales goals relating to them.** Keeping to them is hard. Spending is much easier than making income.

Run your budgeted marketing/advertising campaigns when income is high. Always reevaluate and spend more or less.

Set a hard dollar number goal for how much you must contract for or sell to earn profits, and in what period of time. Do Breakeven and Payback Analysis.

Services are often paid for with an initial fee followed by milestone or hourly fees in clumps, so account for that. Services depend on hours billed. Products are bought and paid in unit quantities at unit prices and may include state sales tax.

Retailers and marketers now offer seller's accounts on their platform, like Amazon, Etsy, eBay, and Walmart, but mostly for products. Angi.com hosts service sellers; Fiverr.com, freelancers. **Sell your products or services on multiple websites and platforms.**

Remember, the world is a services economy.

Companies that once only sold products now sell installation, training, maintenance, warranties and support, upgrades, even deinstallation and removal. **Services equal more than a product sale alone because of greater income possibilities.**

Spending goals

Keep a running monthly record of sales revenue vs. advertising expenses by platform or advertiser and review it often to stay in the black. **One major goal: set a salary target and pay yourself monthly. The first years may be small but set something.**

Other goals are: 1) make enough income to run the business, 2) stay within budget for marketing, promotion, and advertising, 3) put aside $ for a rainy-day fund, and 4) have enough $$ for expansion, or take a loan.

Goals are only effective if:
1. **They're concrete and measurable**
2. **Contain time elements, steps, or deadlines**
3. **Can be monitored and produce desired results**

Research marketing/advertising trends in your industry. Your budget should be a % of your sales revenues.

Rule of Thumb on marketing spends:
B2B (Business to Business), companies spend between 2 and 5% of their revenues. B2C (Business to Consumer), companies, between 5 and 10%.

Selling to companies, government, or organizations with hundreds or thousands of employees means large sales contracts. Just look at Microsoft Office as an example of both consumer users (1.2+ billion), and corporate users (258 million plus). Selling to groups is ideal.

What are you really selling?

> **Everyone hates commercials that interrupt their tv shows or radio listening, and we universally ignore all advertisements and any forms of them. Unless they apply directly to our need or desire.**

R

How do you overcome our reflexive dismissal of most ads?

You are not just selling your service skills, time, or products. "Selling" is more than describing those things or touting deals. **Selling is an emotional, personal appeal. Buying is a mental and emotional decision.**

In the season 1 of Mad Men, ad man Don Draper, played by John Hamm, stated what advertising meant. Human happiness. It's based on one thing, as in the "the smell of new leather seats." **Happiness stems from a love, want, desire, or need that's fulfilled.** Like he said, it may come from the new car smell. But it really comes from honor, prestige, satisfaction, joy—a host of human emotions associated with the item.

In advertising and marketing, you convey the same feeling or emotion: the <u>perception</u> that what you offer is happiness. What you offer makes things "OK" or better. What you offer is gratification. We're all human!

People buy things to satisfy cravings of their body, mind, heart, or spirit. They buy luxuries because they feel like the Joneses or a celebrity. Or they buy strength and security in a Volvo. Or honor, or ease of use, or some other quality. It may smell nice, like Gain or Secret Deodorant.

Good ads attach human qualities.

We see tv ads for cars and trucks every minute. They have envious features like a 430 hp engine in a Ford F-150, automatic braking, heated seats, etc. Or the vehicle has a handsome driver like Matthew McConaughey or a super one like pretty Brie Larson. You see how they love the vehicle. The ad screams, "Be like me."

Bottom line though, the real purpose of a vehicle is to get from point A to point B. We need reliability in our vehicles, like Toyota and Honda make. Quality, comfort, power, ruggedness, prestige, capacity, loyalty, "the smell of leather seats," go along with it. **At a gut level, you are selling the promise it (product) or you (service) work for what the potential buyer or client wants at that moment. You release their urge to buy and fulfill it.**

Sell satisfaction, pride, ease, reliability, and success.

Build your reputation

Store, brand, popularity, and sales come from one thing: reputation. It and you are the most potent sales attractions.

Any store, online or physical that has 5 years longevity is better than one just starting out or only a few years old. We've mentioned the year when many stores opened, and how large they are. Walmart has physical warehouse-sized stores and sells online too. Online-only stores like Amazon, including sellers, has 350 million items delivered physically or digitally.

Small businesses with 1 up to 1,500 employees, medium-sized ones, and large corporate ones, only do well if they:
1. advertise
2. have what shoppers look for
3. are stable and will be here tomorrow
4. have many decent reviews
5. manage themselves, their $$, and employees well
6. are reliable
7. are accessible and easy to do business with
8. have topnotch account, service, and tech support

These 8 equal Reputation. It takes years to build a loyal following and a respected, trustworthy brand. No one said it would be easy, BUT with so many tools and aids, your plans, advice, and info sources, success is almost guaranteed.

Learn how to sell

R

I wasn't a born salesman. Really, I had been a bureaucrat following orders during my career. I didn't have the gift of gab like my friend Bob or Harold Hill in *The Music Man*. As a State of NJ professional meeting with vendors selling us their computer equipment, services, software, or energy, I was on the other side of selling—a cautious, skeptical audience.

Like most potential buyers.

I learned to recognize salespersons' tactics: the Foot in the Door, Take It or Leave It, the Time Deadline, Backtracking, the Salami technique and more. Or the last-minute quarterly discount for signing an evergreen contract, at times postdated.

Learn from videos, webinars, and courses on Selling. Focus on those relating to your industry.

...Three common things mark sales: a known quantity, a time limit, and an associated discount.

Expect the same from potential customers that you do yourself when considering a purchase. Ask questions and check off Likes.

Use what works for you. Ads contain all three. Tailor your campaigns to the right audiences and current exigencies of the situation. Few Inuit buy refrigerators in a snowstorm.

Chapter 36 What you need

Chester says: *You are the tv or movie director yelling, "Action!"*

You are the producer, director, set designer, makeup artist, prop master, casting director, grip and more for your business. No movie can be completed without coordination, organization, planning, and execution. Monitoring and promotion follows.

You must have a webpage

R

We covered this in Volume 1. **This is the 21st Century of Everything Happens Instantly. Primarily, digital, online, or electronic. The future will only be more so.**

You have your business name. Hopefully it's short, memorable and on every piece of media marketing and advertising you construct. **Same with your web address.** You need one major URL to represent you, and the beauty of webpages is that you can have dozens with links to choose.

Initials or a name are great. Consider rodneyrichards.info, my name and site, or like my old RREnergyConsulting described. It's like what happened to George's business when he hung just a one-word sign that said "tutoring."

But if a services business, don't make the mistake I made naming my current LLC "ABLiA." The problem is, it only means something to me, even though Nike seems to do well. But look at the millions they spent in branding!

You don't have $$$ or time to wait to get the word out. You exist to serve people NOW.

It's critical that a services name, i.e. company or webpage, clarifies what you do. You want to attract those who want your service, not sneaker buyers. Retailers almost don't care what their company legal name or moniker is since they are 100% focused on selling the brands/products under their umbrella, i.e. physical and tangible things. Services, especially professional, vary greatly, or specialize like physicians.

You may have started with a free webpage builder like WordPress, but they hit you with the cost of hosting and plug-ins. Zapier lists 8 web builders but check first what purpose they serve. They must have SEO, not like Google Sites. Some are: Yola for simple and no fuss; GetResponse for email-focused; HubSpot CMS for growth; Wix, a good all-around like Weebly; or Dorik for the more experienced.

Better ones with incredible SEO and other features, even merchant services, like SquareSpace, cost $100-$200/yr. You can always transfer your main URL to another web builder platform for 20 bucks. **Start strong. Saturate everything.**

Include a CTA and sales page

Cumulative effects bring recognition and trust that you are who you say you are and do what you say you'll do.

Your website, ads, social posts etc. are worthless—a waste of effort, time, and money—unless you have a Call to Action, known as a CTA. These take many forms, often a question, like, "Want to improve your life?" [click here]. **Your call to action asks the viewer to do something you want them to do.**

There are two major kinds: 1. Information and how to contact you. A phone #, web address, invite or link to find out more, a trial period, sending a sample of your work, or offering free consultations; and 2. a way to buy your product or service.

The most important hook/CTA is a "Sales page."

This is informational, inspirational, or intriguing, interesting, and convincing. Every author knows if a person bites on how the front or back cover of their book looks, then 80% on average will buy it. You know what they say, "A good cover sells books." Likewise, "A good CTA creates the urge to buy."

The Sales Page is compelling, confirms the hook, and can also be the "Checkout." **It's an easy way to purchase directly,** as in a physical store or online, no matter the platform, site, product, or service. It's where you make a sale.

The CTA and the Sales Page/Checkout must be clear, to the point, and easy to understand. It's the clincher. Look at robot checkouts that have taken over grocery stores, or Amazon's one-click "Add to Cart," and "Buy Now." All simple. With phone payment apps and digital wallets, every business has them. **It's KISC: Keep it Simple and Compelling.**

Get reviews and do surveys

On average, positive reviews produce an 18% uplift in sales. The more the better. You get reviews from:

excellent service	complaints
good quality	by asking
referrals	friends/customers

Reviews gain customers and make sales. Positive reviews are magnets. Surveys connect and gain info.

Reviews are more powerful than Likes on social media.
1. **99.75% of online shoppers read reviews** at least sometimes; 91% do so always or regularly
2. 98% of shoppers say reviews are an essential resource when making purchase decisions
3. Nearly half (45%) of consumers won't purchase a product if there are no reviews available
4. 46% of reviewers are likely to trust an online review as much as a personal recommendation

Without reviews, you've lost half your potential buyers. Online reviews are mostly trusted. **Recommendations and reviews create fans who influence others.**

Influencers are powerful allies. If selling services to individuals, ask "How did you like my service?" or "Would you please leave a review?" And then leave a place to do so! Run short surveys everywhere.

You need two types of reviews: those for your business, and those for specific products or specific services.

Find pure gold on Facebook or in social media Comments. Especially with online services or product sales, with their arm's length, non-face-to-face nature, any kudo can grow business and influence others.

Whether on Amazon or any shopping site, buyers' feelings about a product or service are easily checked. Alongside the item or service, there's a rank. Four or five stars is tops. You click a blue number link to read them. Easy-peasy.

When starting a business, you may not have any or only a few, so ask for them! 20 is a start, shoot for 50+.

Surveys

On almost every store receipt there is a survey link. My Dunkin receipts had a survey link and code # to take a survey and get a free donut. I had many yummy chocolate frosted treats, and they got my review.

Easily compose your own surveys and send them out using SurveyMonkey, QuestionPro, Google Forms, Typeform, SurveyPlanet or another. Results are quick. They can be positive or show where you need improvement. **Mix in positive reviews and testimonials onto your website and social media posts. Also, create a survey when visitors click away from your sales page, checkout, or website.**

The Sunk Cost Fallacy

The horse is the business moving forward. The cart holds the oats, water, and apples—the money you draw from your bank account to feed and grow your horse. Without the horse to draw it, your business goes nowhere.

You want meteoric growth? Then, once open, besides operations, you need cash for marketing and advertising. You want steady growth? Use profits to pay for it.

However, don't exceed your marketing budget. Don't flip into a ditch—credit debt or loan hole—thinking sales will pay those costs in time. **Don't fall into "The Sunk Cost Fallacy."**

It's a fallacy in logic. You stick with a losing venture because you've already invested so much time, money, or resources into it. **However, you'll never get what you contributed back.** It could be a Facebook, Google, or Reddit campaign, or a product line that hasn't caught on, or a service that gets no callers. Or the annual cost for a networking organization.

It could be your clinging lover.

You may feel because you've already incurred costs time wise, physically, emotionally, or monetarily, that you need to stick with it to "get your money's worth." However, money once spent cannot be recouped unless it produces more $$ (benefits) in returns than it costs.

Continued spending leads nowhere except to the poorhouse or the nuthouse hoping it will work.

Instead, avoid the sunk cost fallacy and cut your losses when payback is less than the investment. Do a T Chart of pros, cons, and costs. **Don't let emotions or feelings cloud your judgment or hopes to overshadow hard evidence. Or let personal attachments sway you.** Rely on intelligence, experiences, resources, and tools to make better decisions.

Free enterprise is chained to advertising with golden cuffs until a better method is found.

Case studies

Every year your company stays in business, you gain greater credibility, greater market presence and share, and

greater trust with customers and the public. Reliability is a reason company names and perceptions are critical.

You know the company founded by brothers Sam and James "Bud' Walton in Rogers, Arkansas in 1962 as Wal-Mart Discount City. Walmart also owns Sam's Club retail warehouses. As of 2022, Walmart is the world's largest company by revenue, has 10,586 stores and clubs in 24 countries, and operates under 46 different names.

JPMorgan Chase is the largest bank in the U.S. It had meager beginnings as the Manhattan Co. founded in 1799 by Aaron Burr as the second commercial bank in New York City.

DuPont was founded in Delaware in 1802 by E.I. du Pont, a Frenchman with expertise in making gunpowder. Since then, it has made dyes, sweater fibers, even film for Hollywood movies. It holds trademarks like Tyvek, Teflon, Kevlar, and Styrofoam.

Running a business is 99% perspiration and maybe 1% luck.

Companies stay in business centuries because of smart owners, smart managers, and smart decisions. They pivot.

Economies, income, and sales fluctuate, yet well-respected businesses offer stability, familiarity, and satisfaction, day after day. They maintain their brand, service, and follow or set trends. Pass through the valley of instability and climb the mountain of longevity like them. Ride the steed of patience and sacrifice. Thank providence, but don't rely on luck or hopes.

Actual success hinges on planning, preparation, execution, and monitoring. You must be systematic and pivot when necessary.

Chapter 37 Reach your market

*C**hester says: **If you try to reach everyone, you won't. Gear your marketing to those who need or want your product or service.***

Ads generate leads, introduce new products or services, increase foot or online traffic, and attract interest or desire.

But if you shoot off your ad, here, there, everywhere, it's like shooting off a shotgun. Pellets may hit their target, just sting, or miss. You've got to use a more precise weapon.

You've opened your business, physical, online, or both **You are your own boss and are ready for the world to beat down your door.** But, just as every first author knows, there is no "public," no "world" who cares who you are. **The reality is, they don't.** So far, few people may know you exist except well-meaning friends and relatives. You must get the word out.

You need customers.

"The Law of One" is the hardest in life: baby's first steps, earning a diploma, landing the first job, even Mao's Long Marches, one 5,600 miles. Everything is subject to this law. Achieving the first step is the hardest. You've taken the first steps, now you need your 1st, 10th, 100th customer and more.

Catch customers by building relationships. It's called Relationship Management, or CRM, and brings credibility, trust, and numbers. Building a reliable and trustworthy reputation is Reputation Management. These are your foundations. Have your first dollar framed already or buy your frame now. You'll be hanging it soon.

Catch people's eyes, ears, minds, and feelings with news about you, your products, or your services. Thats in your Marketing and Advertising content.

Marketing versus advertising

Marketing is the umbrella that advertising, signs, websites, posts, blogs, newsletters, social media etc. fall under.

Marketing is the activity, set of institutions, and processes for creating, communicating, delivering, and exchanging offerings that have value for customers, clients, partners, and society at large. It's the activity or business of promoting and selling products or services. **You are automatically a marketer of your business.**

Advertising is producing advertisements for commercial products or services. An advertisement is how a product, brand, or service is promoted to a viewership to attract interest, engagement, and sales. **When you produce an advertisement or campaign, you are an advertiser, even if you use others to promote your services.**

Marketing and advertising cost something. How much is up to you. They are not "hit or miss."

Marketing costs much less than advertising. For example, sharing who you are on social media without a fancy ad campaign is free, simple, and direct. Ads are pre-planned, and advertisers use tools or firms to make them look or sound great.

There's a budget. Ads target an audience, whether specific or wide. Make marketing materials and ads yourself at low cost or use others' services or tools. Follow a yearly holiday calendar and take advantage of when shoppers expect sales and discounts. The reality is: with marketing and ads you can invoke interest in those who see or hear it.

Be aware, everyone tunes out or blocks 95% of ads.

Ads are a blip through our consciousness or unconsciousness and aren't remembered until we have a need, want, or desire for that specific thing. Even though ads are all blips, repetition helps them stick in our memory. Then we want to find out more and check it out.

It's a race between obscurity and recognition. How easily and quickly we find what we want determines sales potential. **Offer things people want, need, or desire. Offer access to it quickly and easily.** Google the 10 Best 2023 SCORE.org on-demand webinars for attracting customers and increasing sales.

Refine your Marketing Plan

Marketing channels are <u>where</u> you market and advertise:
- Digital advertisements including yours a/o another's website(s), emails, events, SEO, content a/o influencer

marketing, social media, signage, word of mouth, and traditional marketing.

Markets are largely based on economies. The 8 largest ones by rank are: 1 United States, 2 China, 3 Japan, 4 Germany, 5 India, 6 The United Kingdom, 7 France, and 8 Russia. (Investopedia) Note their huge populations.

"Ah, Horatio, to reach that market, that is the question, is it not?" **Your goal straight out of the gate, depending on what you offer, is deciding whom and where to target.**

R

One section of your Marketing Plan deals with the marketing channel(s) you choose to promote your business, products, and services. To choose well, perform a Market Analysis: What's my industry and competition? Dissect what you offer and understand and package what you are selling. **Determine who wants or needs your services. Create a customer profile.**

"Everyone" is not an answer. Be specific. For example, since my original memoir was about dealing with bipolar disorder, my audience was 4-10 million adult sufferers, near as many caregivers, healthcare providers and institutions, and specifically 23,000 U.S. psychiatrists. **Find the numbers and interests of your customer base. Google likely candidates.**

Today as an editor I can help anyone, even go freelance and write for others. But my optimal customer base is English speakers and writers, users of MS-Word, and writers looking to polish their work for publication.

In your customer profile(s) you may have multiple groups or segments. These folks, defined by type or occupation, age, location, status, language, or interest are your targets.

Write down who they are and what they like. That's what marketers do. When you buy advertising anywhere, match your customer profiles to the advertiser, company, their platform or media, and their users. Selling to your friends only cuts it for a short time, as most authors know who only sell 100 to 150 print books amidst Amazon's 300 million sold annually.

The dirty laundry of retail

Retail sale means a "sale of tangible personal property for a purpose other than resale in the regular course of business. The sale is final once the buyer pays." Sale of services means "furnishing your services to another for a fee." It may or not be tangible, or labor only, but the result is accepted by your buyer under terms you both agree upon, and complete when paid.

Whether selling goods or services, there are options: Sell direct from your website, on your app, accept a direct phone or email order, sell your services or products indirectly from another platform, or from the shelf of a retail store.

You make more $$ selling directly; costs and fees are generally lower. Selling directly, you can offer greater or lesser discounts, set whatever price you want, when you want, with more flexibility. Most sellers do both.

Selling indirectly from someone else's site, like Amazon, Walmart, Shopify, Freelance.com or wherever, means they host and sell your "stuff" or services on your behalf under set terms for a limited time. They get a cut of your sold price for their hosting and for processing your orders, and you make your price higher to cover their fee. **Whomever they are, they reap enormous benefits. They capture and use:**
- **the buyer's name and account information**
- **their email address and phone number**
- **their credit card info for use again**
- **your own money**

Whether buying direct or indirect, the purchaser must set up an account with email, specify a credit card, use PayPal etc.

Do you want that info for your own future ad campaigns, sales, renewals, and contacts? Or do you want the seller platform, not you, to have that advantage and information? Starting out as an unknown quantity, it may be expedient, and cheaper, to sell indirectly on well-known retail or social media site. Consider a move to direct sales when well-established.

Either way, marketing and advertising gets the word out. Ask, "How well do these other sellers do it for me?" and "How much do I pay them to advertise for me?" versus, "How well can I do it myself?" and "What can I afford, either way, or both?"

While doing your research and learning the platform, trial runs and market analytics work best to find out. Market analytics help target your audience to find what consumers needed, wanted, or desired. **Offering that, and ad saturation, should bring increased sales and market share.**

> Good ads attract, inform, and create the urge to buy. Ad campaigns of longer runs work better than one-offs, but both have a place and time.

Big ads aren't sure-fire bets at Pimlico or Churchill Downs or like Super Bowl ads with big payoffs. If using an Amazon, Shopify etc. to sell your things or services, check their buyer user base profile and compare. Do a "T" chart, a decision tree, weighing their larger audiences and the costs and benefits of Direct (you) vs. Indirect (them).

Gotta start somewhere. Growing and making $$ is Number 1. Online is easier and cheaper than opening a storefront. There is a place and need for both.

Truth: Advertisers/sellers such as Amazon, Walmart, Shopify, Facebook et al. have thousands more user accounts, email addresses, and phone numbers than you do. Target their huge ready-made audiences.

It's a big game of sorts and will stay a big game. It's a law of nature and humankind—supply and demand. The purpose of business is to satisfy people's specific needs and wants—for a price. **Needs differ from wants.**

Needs must be satisfied. we need water to live, from a stream, well, tap, or bottle. We're willing to pay for that. What we want to drink, like a Pepsi or Dunkin' coffee, varies with our thirst, taste, access to it, and funds. **Demand varies with the circumstances, supply, and ability to pay.**

Needs are must haves, like donuts and coffee are for me.
Wants are nice to have, like beach homes and hot tubs.

Products and services run the gamut. Needed by some folks, optional or wished for by others, ignored by most. But they can look hard to pass up.

Everyone LOVES deals. We look twice. We stop and reconsider. That's when selling starts.

Whether a storefront or home business, you must give audiences online access to you. First, get their attention: Be positive. Also:
- Make your offers simple, clear, and compelling
- Highlight benefits
- Make deals easy to remember
- Make it easy to buy and pay
- Deliver timely and follow up
- Price must equal perceived value

You must have a target audience or develop one. Achieving brand awareness is only half the battle. Achieving "Sold" is the other half.

The dirty laundry of advertising

You have a choice as a buyer or a seller, you always do: Be fair or be deceptive. You know many ads entice first than hit you with the whammy: the unexpected cost or its too high. You know how many ads are outright fake? About 10-30%.

Companies and entrepreneurs are cunning. Their favorite ploy is to offer a free webinar, podcast, trial, book etc. As you watch or try it out, they offer you an amazing bargain to sign up for their real gotcha: a $5k program to make you a star, or expensive health supplements, or an annual subscription and on and on.

Nothing wrong with that, **if you get something of value and it works**. The only way to know is to get solid, actionable, guaranteed deliverables from them, and to hold their feet to the fire. Ask how many past successful clients or users they have and how long they've been in business before signing on.

Subscribe to the FTC's Consumer Protection Bureau's Alerts. You'll get a good idea of what they find is unfair, deceptive, or fraudulent. Avoid those whether buying or selling.

Primary concerns as an advertiser

The elephant in the room is the high cost for advertising.

The fear is that without advertising, a business won't go anywhere. That's what advertisers want you believe. After all, they make their $$ from businesses that advertise to their users on their platforms by using their media.

Honestly though, ads don't matter except they do. We know a free viral video or tv appearance skyrockets people, products, or services, and sales, through the roof. Look at ABC's World News Tonight's Made in America segments in the last minute that highlights a small U.S. business.

Advertising is specific to media and form, length of time run, fees charged, and cost to produce and run.

Statistica reported that the United States is the largest advertising market in the world, at $250 billion spent in 2020. Individuals, businesses, organizations, even the government pays advertisers. But how do you know if it's a good investment and pays off in sales?

Check the Return on Investment (ROI). You're competing with 4,000 to 10,000 ads that a person sees or hears every day. Does it matter if you have a website, post on social media, buy newspaper ads or radio spots, do targeted group advertising or affiliate marketing, have catchy brochures or business cards, or anything else?

It might not. We can't be sure what medium or message will produce high sales when billions of diverse people see and hear billions of mind-numbing ads. But you have access to their eyeballs and ears, online and off, through either free or paid marketing. And you must have tools that monitor your investment paybacks.

*Marketing isn't expensive; advertising is.
Commerce depends on both.*

We want marketing and ads that work, attract shoppers to our sales page, and the sales page converts them into a sale. It's what churns profits. It's a shame advertising costs a lot and must be repeated so often to be effective.

We can only make <u>informed</u> guesses of what revenue ads will generate. There are billions of people, some have money to spend, some don't, and some will be on the fence. **Reaching more eyeballs and ears creates better odds.**

CTR determines your success with online ads and ROI.

What is CTR?

R

In a physical store, items or products sold, i.e. actually selected, bought, and paid for at the payment terminal, also known as a point of sale (POS) terminal, credit card machine, card reader, PIN pad, or EFTPOS—equal sales. In online stores or websites, whether looking or shopping, a purchase with secure credit card or debit card data, or $$ transfer is a conversion, i.e. a sale. **In the online world, it's called CTR, or Click Through Rate.**

It's the percentage of online viewers of your ad that actually click a "Buy" link and follow through with payment. **As a paying advertiser you are most concerned with CTRs—how many viewers click a sales page link and make a purchase.**

3% to 5% is doing well.

10% to 15% is where you want to be.

Amazon Prime boasts their CTR is 74%, but subscribers to Prime are hardcore buyers, and pay annually for the privilege. **A good CTR means you are on the right platform or media and reaching targeted or interested viewers.** You are spending your advertising dollars wisely.

This only means success if, a) your sales pay for the advertising, and b) sales earn you at least 20% profit. You need both. Ask yourself: What do I really want?

If selling products, you want new customers or recurring ones. Selling services, you want someone to contract with you for your skill and knowledge, provide them with a satisfactory outcome at a fair price, to pay you, and to return.

Bottom line: you are asking someone, a stranger, to trust you, to believe in you, and give you money. Do ads do that? No. But the right marketing or ad at the right time and place opens doors, ears, eyes, or minds. In a word, interest. Success and reputation open them wider. Positive reviews open them wider still. **It's hard to build trust; easy to destroy it. But once earned, it builds incredible businesses.**

Advertisers and marketers know this because they bombard us and saturate the media. They also know we must see or hear an offer 7-10 times for it to stick in our consciousness.

Advertising is five-prong: 1. repetitive, 2. memorable, 3. on different media in unique forms, 4. at different times, and 5. repetitive.

The best ads

Ads cost money, your money. Select places and times by the results they get. Budget for limited runs. Track results. Stop campaigns if not profitable.

On tv and radio, even social media, ads repeat the same basic content many times in the same time slot, like the same ten drug commercials on *ABC World News Tonight with David Muir* night after night. **There are two kinds of ads: spreading company/brand awareness or pushing a specific item or service. Good ads do both.**

Also, ads sometimes tell/show the price. Most don't until you get to their actual sales page. But calling a telephone number is passe; put your web address there. People aren't dumb, or as gullible. They want to know more first.

You will almost never sell to someone who has never heard of you or doesn't like you or what you stand for.

You are your most gifted salesperson because you determine 100% of your marketing strategy. You bring attention to yourself when you post on social media, have a website, write a newsletter or blog, post images, photos, or videos, tweet, upload to your YouTube channel, or do a podcast, radio, or tv spot.

But you don't have time to do all that yourself. You must run your business first. Automated tools and service companies, plenty of them, do much of that for you.

Only pay advertisers for ad space, placement, repetition, and results. Check "Google Ads Transparency Center" for examples. Before creating your ad, check its effectiveness and test it on friends or family. Ask:

- Are they creative? Colorful?
- Do they have reach?
- Are they too narrow or too wide? Which works best?
- Do they reflect current values, mores, or trends?
- Are keyword or phrases included? Are they memorable?

Once the ad is up on yours or another's website or store shelf, be sure to monitor Daily Sales with Analytics. **Only place ads when good analytics are available.**

My wife, Janet, widely experienced in teaching three thousand students in elementary school and college over 30 years, met and talked with parents, union heads, teachers, professors, counselors, principals, secretaries, administrators, and others in her associations. Well-liked by everyone she met and interacted with, it was her mission to remember their names. If it was a chance meeting with an old student, she'd pour through yearbooks until she found them.

She always reminded me: "Get their name," and "Be nice."

Automated tools insert names in the informative email newsletters I receive daily, and they will in yours too. "Catch more flies with honey than with vinegar."

Nothing catches someone's attention quicker than knowing and using their name.

Email is the most effective personal targeting medium with high ROI of 44%. It basically costs pennies to use or automate. It's direct, one to one. Email addresses a person by name. Television may be the most effective with broadcast audiences on the opposite spectrum, but it's expensive. ROI for a TV ad campaign has to be 300-500%.

For online sales, marketing gurus advise: **The real job of pay-per-click ads is to get people to your sales page. Once there, it's up to your SALES PAGE to convince them to buy. That's where your "Buy" link is.**

Nothing can MAKE someone buy your product or service. Not your product or service, not Facebook or Amazon ad campaigns, nothing. Ads only move traffic to your offer and sales page. Do you have an impeccable reputation? A compelling blurb? Excellent reviews? Then you're likely to see sales grow from conversions, the CTRs.

Think of a book on Amazon. Great cover and title? Some buzz? Positive reviews? Fair price? Easy checkout?

If you're spending $$$ on ads and getting no sales, it could be the ad itself, but it's more likely a conversion problem. The ads are doing their job by sending traffic to your sales page, but people still aren't buying.

Spend limited $$ on honing and perfecting your online sales pages and increasing CTRs. Remember too, every company started out with no or few customers and grew because they fulfilled people's needs, wants, or desires. It takes time, resources, including automated ones, faith, and determination. And excellent service.

You will never sell to someone who doesn't know you unless they trust your marketing and advertising—your public "face."

The best ad tells something about who bought from you and more with Analytics. **Don't pay a dime to advertise without Analytics.**

Chapter 38 Target and advertise

Chester says: ***Be creative. Be open. Be flexible. Tweak and reuse what you can—but be fresh. Grow a familiar and satisfied audience.***

There are three types of advertising: personal—face to face; physical media like print ads; and digital/internet media like radio, email, webinars, blogs, social media, pop ups etc.

Wi-Fi and Internet media with billions of users is where you'll reach the largest potential audience with your message. As of October 2023, there were 5.3 billion internet users worldwide, or 65.7% of the global population. Online smartphone/mobile users numbered 6.4 billion in 2022. (Statistica) There's plenty of room.

Whether selling and providing products or services from a storefront, food truck, warehouse, or your basement office, or through Amazon, Shopify, Google Play or another merchant platform, you'll be using computers, printers, electronic POS devices/ checkout robots, your cellphone, and Internet links.

Remember too, an original store location can expand like McDonald's has, now with 40,000+ restaurants since 1940. With one digital online website or access point, you could reach millions of potential customers. Walmart has 255 Mil plus.

Reach the globe, but…

O my Lord! Hundreds of outlets for promotion, marketing, and advertising! How do I choose? How can I pick the right one, spend limited $$, and stay within budget?

Do not run helter skelter into this forest. The trees are many kinds, shapes, sizes, and costs:

Website	Internet ads	Social media
Email marketing	SEO/SEM	Promo products

SMS/text marketing   Retargeting   Radio, TV etc.
GEO fencing   Influencers   Billboards
Wi-fi marketing   Print ads   Public relations

You can't learn their ins and outs of all of them in a few months. Concentrate on a few markets and market channels you've investigated. Invest in what pays off. Invest too in automated tools.

Ads are the lingua franca of commerce and the Internet. They push your brand or service ahead of others in SEO and browser searches. Algorithms and automated tools are the lingua franca of SEO.

The more often you are 'found,' or 'caught,' the higher search engines place you in top results. But without a coordinated, systematic plan, you'll fail.

For example, one statistic shared by Microsoft Advertising stated they have or there are 719 million desktop searchers, 60% of them ages 25-44, 53% married, and 53% college grads.

Spend time, not all your money, planning and refining the tools and options of digital advertising you'll use, because it gets expensive, fast. Like every great author knows: Do the research. Then attack your target audience.

Here's how:

One. List yourself in business profiles on a dozen sites for free, like Google Business or Maps, Yelp, or Bing Places. Many charge a percentage only when you make a sale. Under your personal Facebook Page open a free business-type page, or a specific one, like Amazon and Goodreads have for authors and readers. **Do as many free as you can.**

Two. Google search for products or services like yours and see where they sell. For example, an author can sell books on Amazon, B&N, Baker & Taylor, Kobo, Lulu, Ingram Spark, Digital2Digital, Book Baby, Alibris et al. for a percentage of the sale price. If you are a restauranteur or hairdresser or whatever, list yourself on sites in your industry with other restaurants, hairdressers, etc. Use Whitepages.com, Yellowpages.com, Superpages, Hotfrog, FourSquare and dozens of others.

Those are your baseline, before paying $$ for online/digital advertising. In your Business Profiles, marketing, and ads:
- Use specifics on the platform you advertise on, like Microsoft, Facebook, Google, Yelp, or social media
- Choose the right categories for your product or service
- Track analytics and conversion rates (CTR)
- Show your website address and phone #

Colorful and interesting photos, pictures, graphics, or videos attract the most. Excellent sources of information are:
- HubSpot Blog for marketing and sales with free templates
- Indeed.com's 78 Tips https://www.indeed.com/career-advice/career-development/digital-marketing-tips

Three. Your goal is to capture each visitor's email address and reviews from buyers. Digital advertisers like Facebook, Google, Reddit, Microsoft, Yelp, Spotify etc. want you to sign up and create a campaign. Campaigns cost $$$ and can be for a few days, a week, or months. Effective sales motivators are discounts or coupon codes for customers' sign-ups for services or purchases. Capture their email address.

Sellers often offer three-day giveaways of an item, in hopes buyers connect with them and buy more of their other items at regular price, or just to collect email addresses or reviews.

Advertising takes investment.

You need to pay for advertising from sales income that exceeds expenses. Or try somewhere else.

Four. Remember: <u>Qualities sell.</u> Qualities like Don Draper and the Ad Men sold. Happiness, satisfaction, reputation, reliability, timeliness, and fairness. They appeal to human sensibilities and emotions. **When you sell using human emotions, quantities follow.**

> *Studies show that when a person is happy with something they'll tell one other person, but if not, they'll tell ten.*

Physical advertising signs

> *Advertising costs $$. If it works, continue. If not, stop the bleeding. Measure results in clicks, analytics, inquiries, emails gotten or names, leads, customers, and sales income. Avoid the sunk cost fallacy.*

G

Something that brought in just as much business for our Chesterfield Learning Center for tutoring and learning was a sign that cost nothing.

When an insurance agency moved in a few doors down from us, the manager said she had a red neon OPEN sign she could not use, so she simply gave it to us. It replaced the CLOSED / OPEN cardboard sign we had been using on the door.

This was much more visible at night!

> *Check local ordinances for placing signs near roads or driveways. There are dozens to choose from, many standard and cheap.*

Another consideration was what to place onto the large picture windows in the building's front. The tradeoff of supplying information to the public was cluttering them, making it difficult to see inside. We used one window to advertise our online reading program, but over time realized it was ineffective.

Another window listed the subjects we tutored—all of them. This attracted the attention of several people who walked by.

> *Use decent quality signage. Don't clutter your windows with Flyers taped to them, it looks unprofessional.*

Over the months, Ilene and I had discussed our business name: Chesterfield Learning Center. Although our attorney had given us the idea of the name, instead of using a name with TUTORING in it, we realized people might think we were simply a glorified day-care center. We searched the Internet in vain for a neon sign that read TUTORING.

We found a company that customized signs, and $400 later we received a TUTORING neon sign, which hung in one of our windows, clearly identifying what we did.

It is embarrassing now to realize we spent more than a year before thinking of such a good idea!

We discussed the use of a sandwich sign, which a few other businesses used on the sidewalk just outside their storefront. We decided against it because we didn't want to lay out the money, about $150. The same was true with the large indoor screens to use on the rare occasions we had indoor venues. They cost between $100 and $200. Fancy ones onto which you can project an image ran about $2,000.

However, when we moved to our second location after having established a reading clinic, we bought a large temporary vinyl banner to place on the side of the building.

Another issue was transferring the big lighted CLC sign to a new location. We wanted to move because we experienced trouble with a neighboring business and needed a place with better traffic.

Show people what they want and they will flock to you. *What you do or offer is your major attraction and calling card. Make it simple, clear, and direct.*

G

Yet another large sign we used to promote the Learning Center was a horizontal one seven feet long and five feet high, erected above the press box of an area high school. We had hoped this would be a brilliant investment, because over 1,800 students attended the school at a 90% graduation rate. Surely not only students but also parents would see our sign advertising ACT and SAT tutoring and flock to us.

We paid $3,700 for the sign after the athletic director came to us with the idea. But during the five years the sign was in place, only one person who had seen it visited our learning center—a teacher asking if we needed another tutor. We did not renew.

Rome wasn't built in one year or 1,000. It takes time to gain recognition and grow a customer base. Spread your marketing budget dollars wisely, always measure results, and keep growing.

We considered purchasing a wrap for our car, but at a BNI meeting, a woman who represented a company that created car wraps stated the cost would be $4,000, so we passed.

Further, our principal business car was leased, and I was sure the Hyundai Company would frown on having a car returned after three years with a whole car wrap firmly affixed to it.

Chester the sheepdog was included not only on our new business cards but also on large car magnets. Sadly, I had no feedback on our business recognition due to using car magnets.

However, upon leaving a bank one day, I saw a woman walk past my car, stop, and look at the sign. I think maybe Chester caught her eye?

Signs advertise your brand or name and what you do. They build recognition and familiarity. They provide ways to contact you but don't sell for you. Only relationships do that.

Advertising online

Chester says: **There are five key objectives when advertising online:**
increase Impressions
increase Clicks
increase Top of Search results
increase CTR's (orders)
measure and increase ROI

Digital advertising is bigger than the skyscraper-sized Godzilla who starred in 38 films since his debut in 1954 with his nuclear blazing breath and huge feet. Advertisers back then poured $$$ into television commercials and literally funded the big three, ABC, NBC, CBS, and also "The Big Five" major movie studios of the Golden Age. Globally, digital advertising in 2023 is expected to increase 10% to reach $568 billion.

Online, the most effective advertisements are visual and combined with sound and motion. Movies proved that. Television proved that. YouTube proves it. TikTok proves it. We humans are 80% visual learners, nearly 20% oral learners, with some kinetic (touch) learners. Human attention spans in 2023 are short; therefore, advertisements must be clever, colorful, eye-catching, and memorable. Movement helps.

The average consumer attention span is 8 seconds!

Therefore, when selling a product or service, finding the item fast with a compelling sales page and quick, easy check-out makes the difference between a purchase or not.

Online has the advantage because either by phone or PC, someone can be anywhere globally and doesn't have to travel to a physical store. Online, they see a picture of the product or service, a description, and the price and terms. Delivery is instant, like a software program app download, or the next day on your doorstep.

Or pay $175/yr. for Amazon Prime "free" delivery.

Competition for online eyeballs or foot traffic, choosing a product or service, and conversion to a sale, is tough amid the constant onslaught of ads and 'things' that distract us.

Finding your business, item, or service on the Internet is a crap shoot, unless by exact name match. There's incredible competition for eyeballs and ears.

Businesses want to beat their competitors, first to market, then in sales. Gaining larger market share and presence and becoming ubiquitous and well-liked is every company's mission. **Staying "out front" is this high stakes game.**

Look at Betamax by Sony in 1975. It had 100% of the market. But the player was expensive; customers wanted it cheaper. VHS VCRs came out and Beta went bye-bye. Sony misread the market. Video rental stores popped up, like Blockbuster. Now they're gone; technology changed, and streaming took over.

Customer tastes and cash in their pocketbooks change. Technologies change, as do policies, laws, and regulations. Values and customs too. Fads come and go. It's a moving target along with any local, regional, or national economy.

But in a capitalistic, global, and free market system, competition is given preference. So, get used to it and prepare.

Your business type determines levels of competition. Always check out what your competition does.

My they've made it complex!

As you ponder advertising on those online web giants, it's not as simple as anyone would like. There are so many advertisers like you, and companies trying to grab clicks and CTRs, you have to bid in an auction to show your ads to the best potential customer at the best time.

Facebook Ads and Amazon Ads are big ones. Don't get confused with eBay or Overstock or others, where you list items and buyers bid to buy it. On auction-based ad advertisers like BookBub too, you as the advertiser pay either a CPM (cost per thousand impressions) or a CPC when someone actually clicks your ad. **Remember, neither a CPM or CPC is an actual purchase or CTR.**

There are tradeoffs to using either or both CPM or CPC. Here's a good article on it, and FB and Amazon et al. have extensive explanations. They key? Set a budget and monitor cash out sales.

https://insights.bookbub.com/bookbub-ads-cpm-cpc-bidding/

Market Share

It's always been important to anyone or any company selling anything. It's the portion of a market controlled by a producer or company, even individual, like Taylor Swift, Ed Sheeran, J.Lo, or Beyonce. Their market share is millions of fans and platinum albums sold.

Wikipedia says: Market share is the percentage of the total revenue or sales in a market that a company's business makes up. An example: If there are 50,000 units sold per year in a given industry, a company whose sales were 5,000 of those units would have a 10 percent share in that market.

Now mix-in online too.

There are three aspects: Building market share, keeping it, and expanding it. Everyone uses advertising for all three. For you, as both marketer and advertiser, building your brand right now, look how Walmart Connect, their online omnichannel marketing arm does it. Start small or go big and grow to spend your $$ on platforms or multimedia with large audiences. Better odds, clean and simple.

It's obvious too that just using one means or platform to sell is inadequate, given the difficulty of attracting actual buyers in super crowded, multimedia marketplaces, online and off.

That's why in the opinion of those like Brian Berni of FictionMarketingAcademy.com, an author promotion business, "**email and paid advertising combined are 2 of the most (if not *the most*) important factors** of a successful career in the publishing landscape."

To me as an author, there is no greater competition for buyers online than hoping they'll purchase my book out of Amazon's 32.8 million. Those odds are beyond dismal if I do nothing.

No matter your market, multiple avenues of attack are mandatory, and Brian's points are spot on.

Chapter 39 Advertising nitty-grittys

Chester says: *You can target 100 different ways. Bottom line, build relationships that produce loyal, happy customers.*

Who to target

The audience can be anyone, any group, any demographic, any combination of peoples and groups addressed in 1,000 different ways. Even by Zoom, which we didn't have before 2011.

Your audience is people you want to give your message to because they could use it or they'll like it, or someone told them they would. They used to be called potential buyers. We tried to reach those who may be or become interested in the product or service being sold. **But not everyone is a potential buyer nor a good potential audience.**

To find your best audience, ask:
- What are they concerned about?
- Where do they spend their time? If online, what platforms? What times of day?
- Who do they already listen to, watch, or follow? Can I be similar yet unique?
- What content can I share that will interest them?

For years sellers thought narrower was better, but there's been a sea change. Now many say to go wider, like Matthew J. Holmes, a successful author and entrepreneur.

His reasoning is like the 1958 movie starring Spencer Tracy, *The Old Man and the Sea* vs. success in *The Perfect Storm,* until you know what happens. **Throw out one line and hook to catch one fish or throw out a net and catch thousands.**

Matthew and others have switched to four wide targeted areas:

Location   Age   Language   Gender

Location could be one country or 50. Age is a range, with 18-35 for the young crowd, 35-65 for the more established. Language could be one or All languages, and English is a key one. Gender is just that.

Understand, too, that when setting targeting parameters, Facebook and others are the actual ones who select your audience, and that shrinks over time if too narrow. So, Matthew turns off *Detailed Targeting* on Facebook, and says *Broad Targeting* is the better bang for your advertising buck.

Narrow or broad, times, trends, and algorithms change. Experiment over time, but watch your wallet or pocketbook, and the Analytics and conversions.

Only spend a budgeted amount per campaign. Monitor hits or views via the campaign to sales income from the campaign, the CTRs. The goal is at least 20% profit.

Ad campaigns

When selling services or products from a retailer's online site like Microsoft, Walmart, Shopify, Amazon, or wherever, look at their advertising targeting options. Look too at social media advertising options, Facebook and Reddit being two.

Because big advertisers want your ad commitment they offer a free consultation with one of their advisors. Call them and be frank about your plans and learn at the same time.

Remember that no matter where you pay for advertising, paid advertisements get precedence on search engines. Advertisers want you to commit $$ to a campaign. Once they get it they prioritize your ads and their frequency. It's a simple but lopsided quid pro quo. They rake in guaranteed $$ from you, while your sales are completely up in the air.

Your goal is to sell more, but when paying for any kind of advertising, your objective is to match how well sales do during that period of advertising with your advertising costs. That's where Analytics comes in. These sites should tell your quantity of sales, by day and item. Unfortunately, they can't always. This is when you must pay attention to the fallacy of sunk costs and juggle your budget for ads, your breakeven point, and your profits.

Time is your friend or your enemy here, deciding whether to continue advertising or to stop. Watch sales carefully, they tell the story.

Amazon vs Facebook

Chester says: ***Advertiser platforms are not alike, nor are their markets. Know whom you are selling with. Set a daily budget.***

Need we say, "Don't fall for promises?" No advertisers' results are guaranteed, in fact, they disclaim them all. Your money is precious and limited. You know too that deals sounding too good to be true are snake pits.

Only stay with an advertiser as long as their results satisfy you. Don't be Mick singing, (*I Can't Get No*) *Satisfaction* no matter what incentives they offer to stay on with them. That said, take their dollar credits when starting fresh, practically all offer them like Redditt.

R

As a writer, I subscribe to writing tips, marketing, and publishing newsletters for free. Entrepreneurs offer their plans, books, programs, courses, consultations, and services for thousands of dollars to help writers succeed.

Check for similar entrepreneurs in your industry and learn from them. Use their free tips, newsletters, blogs, and facts to see trends and what's happening in your industry. See what they're selling, and how. Learn and copy their techniques and put your own stamp on your offerings, posts, and advertisements. You'll also find great tools to use or buy.

But be careful before committing $$ to any program. Only sign up if, 1. it has a proven track record, 2. it's clear what will be done, or not, when, where, and how, 3. you can afford it, and 4. results can be analyzed.

Highlighting or showing your other related services can be another way to make income via affiliate marketing, so look for opportunities.

One authorpreneur I admire is Derek Doepker. In one of his posts, he compared advertising on Amazon vs Facebook. His opinion is:

Amazon ads:
- May be easier to start for the novice and more cost-effective on a small scale
- May appeal to those already there, since they are looking for something to buy already
- Perhaps higher conversion rates from searching first, finding something that fits, to buying
- May tend to be profitable when first starting out.

A good Amazon average conversion rate is 10-15%. On Prime, higher.

Facebook ads:
- Many, many users are there to share what's important to them, or for distraction or connection. They are usually not there to necessarily buy
- It's a different mindset than Amazon purchase searchers. Many FB users are having fun expressing themselves.

- Ads may be easier to scale once dialed into your niche, tribe, or fanbase.

The FB 2023 conversion rate was estimated at 9.21%

However, know what your advertiser is guaranteeing. Amazon, for example, is not guaranteeing people will buy from you. If you advertise with them, you are assuming you should get more clicks on your sales page, or impressions, or ad clicks. **They are selling potential clicks, like impressions for example. Most charge cost-per-click (CPC), or pay-per-click (PPC), like to your website landing page or an item for sale. And you pay whatever their terms are.**

Google and other ads

Check Google. Their average conversion rate for Google Ads across industries in 2023 was 7.04%. (Source: WordStream)

They may be the most robust advertiser, and sophisticated. They've been around since 1998 and have perfected dozens of functions and capabilities. Check them out at ads.google.com. Scroll to the bottom of their pitch screens for specific topics and research how they handle Analytics.

Google offers up to $500 credit for signing up and advertising. Most other advertisers do too, like a $200 credit on Reddit. Take advantage.

Don't ever forget that these sites, Google, Facebook, Reddit even Microsoft and others, make some or most of their income from advertisers and their commitments. Do your homework before spending $$ on any platform.

The first rule is to know why their specific users are on their platform. Each platform has:
- A unique audience/demographic
- Proprietary algorithms
- Different categories, steps analyzing what to buy, and requirements for what can be specified
- May have a direct vs indirect means to purchase (immediate vs. prior steps first)
- Reasons why the users like to use it

"Immediate" are ad pages that go direct from product choice to checkout, usually a button on the same page. A prior step might be having to open an account on that platform. Entering credit card data is also a prior step, and buyers can back out before completing the purchase. An automated email follows up by asking why they're leaving, sometimes offering a discount. Do this if selling direct from your own webpages.

Ad creation tips

You need to catch attention online with ads and marketing. Proven ways to do that are to use:
- The Rule of Thirds and the Golden Ratio
- Color psychology/good graphics
- Testimonials, positive reviews, and endorsements
- Placement and typography (fonts and white space)
- Clear visual paths leading to the sales page or checkout
- Association with what's known or understood
- Emotional, human appeal; "Talk with me"
- Optimize the tricks of the media you use
- Consistency

The Rule of Thirds pertains to photography and breaking an image into thirds, i.e. the subject or message does not have to be dead center. Balancing makes it eye-catching and pleasing, the Golden Ratio. Limited text or graphics surrounded by white space catches glances best. Don't cram them in.

Clean links to your sales page(s) and checkout/CTA are #1, and/or to your phone # or website/webpage.

5 key features in posts or ads

These stick out in the best social media posts, ads, marketing materials etc., regardless of the number of photos/graphics or words used. They are:
1. The name of your business or brand
2. Primary text
3. The Creative – perhaps a graphic or photo

4. Headline, and underneath, description
5. The Call to Action (CTA) button

Chapter 40 Refine marketing

*C*hester says: ***The Five Rs of Marketing and Advertising are proven elements used by effective marketers.***

A good salesperson like con artist Harold Hill in *The Music Man,* is always "on." He took advantage of opportunities and created openings to achieve his goal: sell band instruments and uniforms to everyone in town, keep the money, then split.

Don't be a con artist, but always be "on" like him, taking advantage of marketing opportunities wherever you are and in whatever you do. Keep these Five Rs of Marketing and Advertising in mind:

Research: Who will benefit from my services or products? Whom might that be? Every marketer and advertiser needs to know the demographics of their target audience.

Relevancy: Stay relevant. Know the trends. Create what relates to customers' lives and what they may not find somewhere else, or they will go elsewhere.

Relate: Create a community, a tribe or fanbase. Help your customers share with each other. User forums, customer support, and reviews do that. Sharing excites people.

React: Provide content for your users, like updates, blog posts, FAQs, or newsletters. Help them understand your services, products, and their benefits.

Reach out: Reach out to your contacts, ask them to share and create buzz. Make sure your customers know what to expect from you. Respond when contacted.

Market around your brand name and offerings. Be consistent with coloring, graphics, photos, and logos in your ads.

You need good graphic generators and photos to create your marketing materials. Check these for photos, some free, to add to any post or ad: Getty Images, Freepik, Shutterstock, Pexel, Picsart, iStockPhoto, Pixabay, Flickr, Wikimedia Commons, Creative Commons affiliates, Google Images, or Nappy.

Caution: Only use "Public Domain" photos, commercially licensed ones, your own, or those you have permission for. Make sure you do not break copyright laws or 'lift' from copyrighted materials. Photos used for commercial purposes usually have license fees. Do not use song lyrics; they are all copyrighted, although titles are not.

Design software tools are important to have. Look at Corel Paintshop Pro, Adobe Creative Cloud products/Photoshop, InPixio, AdCreative, and Fotor et al. For Art Creators, check Dall-E 2, Midjourney, Cralyon (free), or Jasper Art. Like all software apps or programs offered today, some have free versions or free trials, and premium features cost extra, with monthly or cheaper annual plans. AI adds boatloads of creative options to all of these tools.

Don't hire a graphic artist every time you want to create or modify an ad, flyer, brochure, business card, bookmark, rack card etc. Outlets like Vistaprint and 4Imprint exist for you to do the design, printing, and publishing yourself for physical imprint and digital marketing products.

Canva has tons of templates, free or premium, for designing digital ads, flyers, cards, and more, as does Suno.ai, Adobe Express, Visme, Stencil, Snappa, or Design Wizard. Save your work as a jpeg and use it repeatedly.

Adobe Acrobat DC, and Gimp.org and IrfanView, both free, are powerful image or document modification tools and convert items to or from many different formats, like pdf to jpeg.

Marketing services and products

> *You don't have to spend a lot trying things out. There's freebies and trials. Experiment, get comfortable, find what works for you.*

Rule #1 is to believe, "Yes, I can do this." With basic intelligence, research, time, the right tool, and trial and error, you can teach an old dog new tricks, and they'll also remember the old ones.

Good information is a click away. You can weigh pros and cons before jumping on a bandwagon and being committed monetarily. HubSpot, a business resource, has excellent articles at https://blog.hubspot.com. They look at the Marketing Process as 3 spokes of a wheel:

> **Attract attention and potential customers to you**
> **Engage them, get known, and get chosen**
> **Delight them and keep them coming back**

Tools to Attract or catch attention are ads, content, video, blogging, email, or social media. Tools for Engagement are lead management and flows, email strings, podcasts, webinars, conversational bots, or sequences. Tools for Delight are, once again, email, Smart Content, and marketing automation.

Where to begin, what to try and, for how long? And how much should I spend?

Look at various tools and products. Try out ads in steps and bites, like that first journey or Subway hoagie. Draw a timeline. Reflect on failure or success, refine your strategy, and adjust accordingly. **To succeed, you must be firm in principle, flexible in details.**

Use AI tools

Content is king.

The top 15 most admired Madison Avenue ad firms crave content. In business, government, news outlets, media outlet, the entertainment field, everywhere, they need content. News outlets live for it. The 2023 WGA and SAG-AFTRA strikes showed what happens when writers and actors are sidelined.

Until AI came along, generating text or other content, whether brainstorming or writing or composing, was time-consuming. Now enter a query in ChatGPT, CoPilot or 10 other dotcoms and within a second receive paragraphs of written copy.

However, AI content must be checked and verified because it could be false, skewed, or copyrighted material. The New York Times is suing ChatGBT over copyright infringement. Movies like *The Terminator* and its evil AI network Skynet should frighten us. AI must be adapted or modified for the intended audience and serve that audience.

AI produces content faster and draws from vast repositories of data. Think of AI for your business as a baker thinks of leavening agents for baking, like yeast, baking powder, and baking soda. AI has access to billions of ingredients and can make what you want quickly. In your AI query, describe what you need specifically in terms of questions or instructions.

A specific marketing campaign? Ask, "What's the best way to market my _____ to Generation X?" No problem.

Forbes pointed out these AIs:
- Google BARD or its new name Gemini
- Microsoft's Sydney or newer one, Copilot
- ChatGBT-3.5 or -4 (highly ranked)
- Dall-E 2 for images, photos, drawings, paintings
- Stable Diffusion 2 for text to images
- Lumen5 for video creation
- Soundraw, music generation
- Podcastle for audio recording
- Murf, for text-to-speech

There's also Watson X, Bing AI, Dragonfly, YouChat, and Poe by Quora. **Use AI queries but verify the facts.**

> *The rule of all rules: What you put out there in writing can haunt or bite you. No, no, no typos.*

The goal of AI in marketing is to increase speed, automate manual tasks, improve ROI, and track campaigns. HubSpot points this out too, and AI helps with media buying, creating chatbots, automating email campaigns, forecasting sales, improving customer experience, and finessing SEO.

AI results and processes save time, the most precious thing on Earth everyone treasures besides their children.

G

We ran out of the second iteration of our Chesterfield Learning Center color trifold brochures, which I had created using the computer and jpeg photos. So, we opted instead to utilize rack cards, which were made of sturdy stock $3^{1/4}$ by $8^{1/4}$. They were smaller, less expensive, forced us to be more succinct, and offered customization of each card to target specific clients.

This resulted in four cards: those seeking preparation for a nursing exam, SAT and ACT tests, high school and elementary courses and exams, and those interested in our reading clinic.

See Appendix B for what the rack cards looked like. Simple to create on the PC, print in color on thicker card stock, and easy to hand out or pick up.

Be aware that mass opportunities to hand someone a physical something are limited on the Net. But everyone loves information in this Information Age. Share your knowledge or insights and people will follow, hence the popularity of blogs, newsletters, social media, and videos.

Fun and stories capture us most.

Automation

You want to automate processes, but it depends what you want to do, and how much you are willing to pay. There are software aids or programs that do everything, but they can be time-consuming to learn and configure.

We all go through learning curves. **Start slow and grow.**

Online or app-based automated software marketing tools use AI help with advertising, social media, and email. Their benefits outweigh costs. They:

- Save time from doing things manually
- Save time in following leads effectively
- Save $$ with fewer resources needed to perform tasks
- Support personalization
- Help in prioritizing and testing
- Take advantage of opportunities
- Manage schedules and workflows
- Automate and personalize email messages

Starting out, MailChimp.com is simpler for an email handler. However, its advanced features can be overwhelming. MailerLite is a competitor.

ActiveCampaign.com is entirely geared toward small business. It's a robust platform.

Constant Contact is a mini-CRM and email handler.

Drip.com focuses on email marketing. Configure behavior-triggered workflows to move customers through your funnel. **A funnel directs viewers where you want them to go. There is no confusion or hesitation. As a seller, you always steer the course.**

HubSpot.com will control your entire small business sales and marketing. It is rich software, but the learning curve and price may be steep.

InfusionSoft.com takes an all-in-one approach and includes CRM, email marketing, ecommerce and more.

Subscribe to their free newsletters. Marketing automation gives powerful advantages, but only if set up and configured properly. You've seen automated scripts each time you received an email newsletter. Or, when you're ready to click out of screen or an ad, and a pop-up appears with an even greater discount. Copy and steal their methods and processes, but not their exact words. Imitation is easier than creating from scratch.

Brainstorming

Chester says: *The only constant is change. Don't get in a rut. Explore new ideas. Coddle existing customers, bring in new ones, and build relationships.*

G

I had purchased Chester, a small-sized synthetic sheepdog, at a Unitarian Universalist Fellowship fundraiser auction. The moment I saw it/him up for auction, I thought, "George, that can be the mascot for our business."

Research had informed me that brand recognition is vitally important, as seen with Nike's swoosh, McDonald's arches, the Mercedes logo, etc. We felt our current logo of a flattened book was not unique and attracted little attention.

An icon of a sheepdog needed a connection to tutoring, so I named the dog Chester and invented the phrase "Chester to the Rescue."

Running a business is being interesting and pleasing to customers and potential customers. If you aren't open to change and new ideas, you will fold.

Before 2010, words and texts were great, but pictures and photos, jpegs, command more attention. Then the ease of taking videos with smartphones overtook those. In 2011, with the Chesterfield Learning Center, we were between traditional marketing and advertising and the new wave—pictures and videos.

Beside Chester, I often brainstormed promotion ideas. One was to draw in excellent students by capitalizing on the fact that I was an alumnus of the well-respected University of Virginia. I hoped this would raise our status as a great tutoring institution.

I contacted the university and asked if I could promote it by offering information about their school at our Learning Center and on our website. The alumni association was pleased to honor my request and provided a booklet and other data.

Unfortunately, this idea did not result in recruiting more students, but gave parents something to read while they waited for their children to be tutored.

We also tried Constant Contact. To entice summer students to use our services, we used the cliché "summer slide" to little effect, perhaps because it was overworked. Instead, we came up with a summer tutoring slogan to "Catch Up, Keep Up, Get Ahead." We didn't want to be known as glorified babysitters.

Don't stop trying ideas and coming up with new things. It gains more attention and larger success.

G

Another marketing idea we had was fun to invent, even though it did not bring in students. One day, while sitting in my car, I looked at the indicators of various gears by the shift lever and mused on how a car went from low to high speed.

Likewise, through tutoring, one could move from low grades to high grades. I took a photo of the gear markers and replaced the numbers and letters with grades.

The gear shift mechanism even had + and – on one side of it!

However, it got taken too literally. One person said the gears didn't work the way I envisioned. Disheartened, Ilene said to me, "People don't think the way you do."

That doesn't stop being creative and trying new things. **People are different and need to see things in different ways for one of them to connect.**

Don't let setbacks or failures grind you down. One person's opinion may be ignored, but if others agree with them, pay attention.

Funneling

Marketing pundits talk about funneling, or CRM on steroids, which has been around for decades. Customer Relationship Management is the point when you reach out, get buyers, and maintain the relationship into the future. **Funneling directs them where you want them to go right from the get-go.**

Tools such as AI, schedulers, automated email scripts, texts, and ad creators help do that, and they build and cement the relationship along the journey. **They reach your target audience, connect and reel them in to your sales page, convert, and achieve recurring sales and recurring revenue.**

Once you have a lead, don't let them get away. That's why newsletters are so popular. They are mostly automated content with text you supply sent to warm bodies. They maintain relationships beautifully and are sales avenues par few.

Look for funneling guidance or help at Google CRM, Funnels, and Modern Marketing. There are dozens to pick from and some cost a pretty penny. Zoho, Zendesk, Keap, Pipedrive, and Salesforce are others. They can get expensive, but their tools are extensive.

However, funneling relies on traffic and leads. Traffic is of two kinds: cold or warm. Cold is a stranger. It's harder to convince one to buy from you. Warm traffic is someone who knows you, or someone referred to you by your contacts or customers. **A warm contact is easier to convert to a buyer because they already have a reason to trust you.**

A referral or recommendation is gold.

Cross-Promotion

As a startup trying to reach out to as many as you can, don't forget other entrepreneurs and solopreneurs like you. **Cross-promotion has three aims: Gain a larger audience, Make sales or friends, and in a way, Grow your email list.**

Say you have 100 customers or newsletter subscribers, or even friends on your email list. You probably know others that do to, probably more. Simply offer to mention them or their product or service (as long as it's not direct competition), to those on your email list, in return for them offering to mention you and what you offer to those on their list.

No obligations or payments like affiliate marketing, but it's an easy way to grow and spread the word and catch some fish.

Ride the sales wave

Are you a sideline business, happy where you are and with your time commitments? Or do you want to expand? If so, you need more cash and to spend more time managing the business, not just be its primary services provider yourself. **Many businesses fail here. You need a plan either way.**

Small businesses fail because of the owner's/ operator's poor transitions from "doing the work" to "managing the work" or managing others, especially when sales are strong, and work is hectic. Pause and regroup.

If sales are hopping, profits allow it, and you can handle it, spend more $$ on reaching out and/or advertising. Review sales and analytics daily. "Make hay while the sun shines."

When your popularity or sales are jumping like kangaroos in the outback, capitalize on the spurt like a racehorse hearing the starting bell at Belmont Park and feeling the jockey's whip. Ride the 30-foot Waikiki wave like an ISA surfer. Milk it like a Jersey Holstein cow into your profit bucket like your hungry children depended on it. You may need capital to expand advertising and time to manage it.

Although, prepare for when the Kingda Ka rollercoaster stops, and the ride is over. When the farmer sees dark storm clouds appear, he or she pulls the farm animals back into the barn until the sun rises again. It will.

You need funds to expand, to take advantage of sales spurts, to improve your offerings and business, and even hire staff. **You need a rainy-day fund or the ability to borrow in troubled times.**

Like a Boy Scout, "Be prepared." We all have unforeseen challenges or circumstances that pop up. As far as change and market conditions go, its evolve or die.

Chapter 41 Shutting Down and Restarting

Chester says: *Face facts. Don't use just feelings and instincts to make business decisions. Use evidence, feelings, instincts, and intuition equally.*

R

I had started my first business, RREnergy & IT Consulting, two months after I retired in 2009 in a flurry of excitement, sure that senior executives I knew would want to hire my expertise.

I spoke to a dozen close potential state agency clients until blue. All too hesitant to commit. I hadn't gotten one paying client but had emailed out free tips in blog articles weekly. My WIX website was homemade, static, and—**boring.** However, when I Googled my name or company, both were prominent on Google's first page.

My home-based office out-of-pocket costs were low, mostly for a PO box, copying, and software programs. No real dent in my retirement income. But after three years with no sales or prospects, my passion and hopes evaporated.

I told Janet, "Hon, I'm not getting anywhere with RREnergy. I'm going to dissolve it."

"Well, okay Rod, but any clue what you'll do to keep busy?"

"Remember, when I wasn't doing anything after I retired, and you suggested I write my memoir or something?"

"Yes, you've said you've been working on it."

"Well, I'm nearly done. It's called *Episodes*. I'm going to publish it."

"Oh. Do I get to read it?"

"Of course. I'm going to have Staples print a draft copy."

Deadpan, in a voice full of dread, she adds, "I can't wait."

I left it at that....

Changing gears

"The only constant in life is change."—Heraclitus, 500 BCE
"It's evolve or die...."—Craig Charles

R

In 2010 my son Jesse invited us to lunch at a Manhattan restaurant and had a surprise. Janet and I tried guessing. Rachel pregnant? A new job? We enjoyed the meal, on him, and our visit, excited to hear his news. Then he pulled out a book titled *The Secret Peace.* He was the author!

Jesse even published it himself on Amazon. I was hooked. I had to learn how to polish and publish, and Amazon was becoming the biggest platform for books. I opened an account on CreateSpace and gobbled up their How to's. I Googled the Library of Congress, ISBNs, and everything on self-publishing and authorship. I bought used books on writing and attended workshops by Murphy Writing, my friend Peter's company.

I realized I loved to write prose and poetry. I also wanted my own publishing company, an LLC. I needed a name.

I had learned by then an important lesson writers and poets adhered to: **telling turns readers off. I needed to show, not tell, a cardinal rule of life and business.** If I was to sell and grow my business, I had to show what I could do.

A new enterprise

R

I dissolved RR Energy Consulting. The steps to start my new publishing business were easy. I had gone through them before. The first thing was a name—ABLiA Media LLC? I Googled it and it didn't pop up taken. I created a Gmail account, 1950ablia@gmail.com .

Other steps followed online:
1. Obtained a free federal EIN number from IRS
2. Filed the New Jersey REG 1 application for $250
3. Opened a business bank account, got a credit card etc.

Your business is probably well past these steps now.

I drafted my 2-page Articles of Incorporation. A friend and Notary Public witnessed it. I filed a copy at home and Janet got one copy as a non-controlling member except in emergencies.

Your Articles are likely done.

By December 2012, ABLiA Media was a viable entity with me as Principal. I was my own boss again!

But in hindsight, ABLiA was the worst possible name.

It conveyed nothing about who I was or what I did. It only meant something to me. It wasn't "brand memorable." Worse, it was barely pronounceable! Janet called it "Abulia."

Today, Big Ideas for Small Business notes Rocket Lawyer has AI tool Rocket Copilot to find or make a no cost memorable business name.

Cute names are weird. You don't want that.

I called Spud, a friend and master of all trades, to photograph the cover pic for my first memoir—my silhouette, arms raised to the moon. He came over, snapped the pose, and composited a fantastic cover, just what I wanted.

I bought my ISBN and got the free LCCN. I was ready. I uploaded it all onto Amazon's CreateSpace in early 2013.

In 2 days, I was a published author!

> *Having a product or service to sell is the first part. The second part is catching attention through marketing. The third is selling it.*

Although I had loved IT, energy, and the environment, I was now free to follow my genuine passion—writing. I began creating essays and poems. The path to becoming an editor and publisher of others' works followed.

My first marketing materials were a business card and bookmarks from Vistaprint to handout. I was on my way again. A new, different, exciting, and, as it turned out, a crowded path with other writers doing the same thing.

- Life [and business] is a journey, not a destination.—Ralph Waldo Emerson

- They always say time changes things, but you actually have to change them yourself.—Andy Warhol

- Only the wisest and stupidest of men never change.—Confucius (Kong Qiu)

Chapter 42 Targeted sales techniques

Chester says: *Strong products or services with more relevant marketing wins.* ***Address receptive audiences.***

In business you need a strong product or service. By strong means value, to a few who pay more, or to many who pay a little and it adds up. **The goal of marketing is to make what you offer relevant to a potential buyer.**

Once it's been purchased, the buyer is pleased with its or your performance and tells others. Then a tribe is born.

Reach actual needs

G

We gave rack cards highlighting our Learning Center nursing courses to a local hospital with a nursing preparation program. Ilene arranged with a caterer to provide light food and drink to their staff, and we visited them at their training center.

This was ideal: going where our customers were. We had proof the cards were effective because prospective nursing students came into the learning center with a card in hand.

Go where your customers are, in person and on media.

At the center we also offered a proprietary online reading program called Reading Plus that I had used effectively with college students while I was a professor at DeVry University.

The company accommodated my need to sign up one reader at a time after the business got underway in 2012; however, within three years the company required us to sign on a minimum of six students at a time, which would have cost several hundred dollars more, so we stopped using it. It was "a nice to have," but not integral, and we worked around its loss.

"Nice to haves" are indeed nice, but if the cost is too high or payback low, let it go.

This was unfortunate for our students who used it, though, for they could access the program at home and at the learning center, and I could monitor their progress from anywhere. But because of its limited use, we felt we couldn't pass on part of the cost to students who might use it.

The fee per student would have increased 250%.

We charged a nominal fee for each student, amounting to only a few dollars more per lesson than it cost us. We viewed the program as a supplement, never as a replacement. I spoke to a representative at the company and explained how pleased we had been with the program to date.

However, experience taught us that few parents in our area would pay the increased cost of using the program if we raised our rates. Regardless, we were told no exceptions to the new rates could be made.

R

Starting my energy consulting business in 2009 in a faltering economy had not been wise. Capital investments were scarce.

Nearly 1 in 5 U.S. businesses fail the first year. Do your research. Don't be one of them.

However, thousands of business types succeed under adverse conditions. I had to admit either I wasn't a good salesperson, or circumstances were against me. I reflected on why RREnergy failed, and what to do differently for ABLiA Media. My message then had been about saving money by installing energy conservation measures in New Jersey's 4,000 state owned buildings. It hadn't worked.

We can reflect on why things work or don't.

Facility managers, like Scrooges, were pinching pennies back then in the down economy while dollars in electricity cost savings went down the kwh drain. **My messaging wasn't correct, I hadn't reached the right people, or my timing was terrible.**

Then I remembered what my best friend, Bob Harris, had once said.

He's a terrific public speaker, loquacious, informative, inspirational, moving his audiences to tears, even me, a hardnose. He had addressed thousands of diverse children, youth, adults, and senior adults in many countries. Funny as hell and silver-tongued, he had hundreds of jokes memorized and hundreds more on index cards.

A master at timing, audiences loved him.

He said, "To be effective, the speaker must have the right message for the right audience. It's that simple. I can have a brilliant speech, but if the audience isn't right, the message goes nowhere."

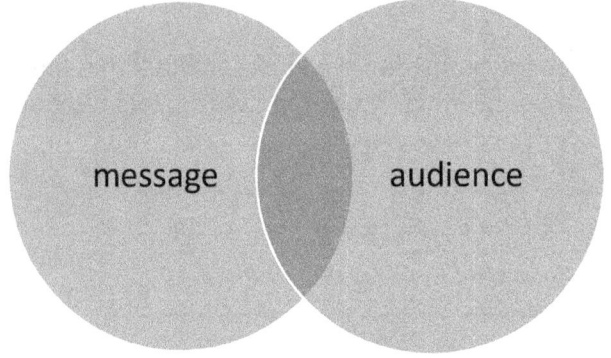

The message is effective when audience and message overlap.

In 1964, communications guru Marshall McLuhan said, "The medium is the message."

Your audience has to be receptive, or it won't work. Not every audience is. They have to looking and are ready to catch the ball you throw toward them. The type of "ball" must fit their expectation.

A phone call, posts on social media, website pages, business cards, ads, flyers, blogs, newsletters, emails, or personal contact are all "baseballs." You're throwing it to those with gloves— an interest, desire, or need to catch it.

Target your marketing. Little else works as well.
Targeted means profile your "receptive audience."

For ABLiA Media to work, my book, or whatever I morphed into or produced, had to focus on reaching receptive audiences.
However, no one, no business idea or name, no business card, nor any ad, is guaranteed to attract someone to take the next step and buy. It's a combination of steps. A process.
Sometimes we drive past that glaring billboard 20 times before being interested enough to call its 800 number.

You are the Sower

You need enough seed clients to pay for business operations, including salary, and 20% profit.

R

Remember Christ's parable of the Sower in Matthew 13?
Throwing your message indiscriminately will produce fewer results. Spread your message on fertile ground. The richest soil is those looking for you. But it depends on what you want in deciding how broad or specific your targeted audience is. For personal services, you physically only have 16 to 18 hours a day to be productive, and we need coffee or tea breaks.
Products sell second by second day and night, online and in stores. Therefore, the rule is simple: Spend your advertising budget reaching that fertile soil.

The best example of guaranteed sales is the grocery store. What you need to eat or drink is right there.

You've been in a grocery store or food mart countless times. It and agriculture are the backbone of civilization. At he grocery store shoppers have choices or no choice. The milk in my ACME is only one brand. If I need it for cereal that's my only choice. However, the cereal aisle holds 30 brands, flavors, colors, and textures. Your product or service is the same way in this retail sales world. You are or are not the sole source for the item. Even if you are, that only lasts so long.

Your audience is not captive anymore, like I am in ACME for milk, especially not online with DoorDash and GrubHub.

Your overarching goal is to bring an audience to you that wants you, or find and reach that audience. Traditionally, that meant running a sale with a discounted price from the normal everyday price. Sales attract. <u>But in any grocery store, price is secondary if one is hungry.</u>

Offer payment plans and choices. Offer installments on bigger purchases. Offer incentives and multi-year and volume discounts. Offer limited time windows, one time only deals, or limited quantities.

When hungry, the urge to buy is a powerful motivator.

When pitching your baseballs to those in your customer profiles they are potentially hungry. Rely on that.

Email reaches out directly

Most agree on the benefits of email, but only if it has value to the recipient. Many say it is the most effective outreach method. It is effective at building relationships and sales because:

- It's personalized. Everyone reacts positively to seeing their name in the Subject field and body of the email
- It targets an audience. You control who messages go to
- Increases brand awareness, leads, and sales
- Generates traffic with feedback and replies
- It's automated and timely, perfect for campaigns
- Provides value and information. Encourages responses
- Builds a community who help cross-promote

- You own your contact lists
- It saves time with automated scripts and is cost-effective
- Includes one or more offers or programs etc.

Email also has that 44% ROI.
Did you see automated scripts? Easily set schedules and immediate responses or email follow-ups based on actions or non-actions by users on your website or a merchant services platform, i.e. automated funnels. Define those to be contacted by group settings in your email software per type of campaign.

Check this Zendesk article for the 13 most popular email automation and script-building software providers: https://www.zendesk.com/sell/features/email-productivity/

HubSpot reported that 77.8% of users check their email inbox over five times a day, while 18.1% of users check their inbox 2-4 times a day. With emails coming through phones, iPads etc. you don't have to be at a PC.

Plan your email campaign in advance. Onboarding sequences follow up with the recipient, with the same idea as the original, said slightly differently, or repeated. They can be automatic, set to run days at a time, one after the other. One email per day is the limit or you'll alienate the recipient, unless it's a reminder for a webinar, limited time offer etc.

The most important line on any email sent is the Subject line. It must be catchy but not snarky. It must be engaging or entertaining, even funny. Be pointed yet raise interest, clever even too, but not vague nor misleading. **Deliver what you suggest will be inside your message. Show an attitude of generosity and service.**

Google's Gmail, AOL Mail, Zoho Mail, Optonline, Yahoo Mail, MS Outlook, and others, and the automated script providers, have limits on email sends. A free Gmail account is 500 daily and 250 per message sent. You can pay for more.

Rules are changing. Effective February 1, 2024, Google Gmail and Yahoo Mail limited accounts to personal emails only, with bulk email senders required to have a domain sending address. Others will too.

Check your website host/provider for a URL dotcom-based email address to use. Most offer one as part of your subscription. Then copy and download your contacts to it.

Custom domain email names cost more, like Google Workspace. Without your own DMARC-compliant email domain you won't be able to send bulk emails. Every email you send must have to have an Unsubscribe link or process.

It takes time to set up, but then forget it. Automated emails, surveys, and campaigns really connect, save you time, and are effective.

Ecommerce automation

Automation tools respond to what a user or viewer on your direct sales site does or doesn't do. You control the text and sequence, but these tools also have templates and canned personalized messages. They follow the course you as the captain set.

The first automated message to viewers is a Welcome. A post purchase email with order confirmation, receipt, shipping info, a/o survey is warranted. An abandoned cart email goes out if a viewer doesn't buy. You might have an interest-based email showing other items or services related to your main offering. Amazon and others are leaders in that.

Sending an interest-based email built on what the viewer clicked shows them other things they may like. Send out a product or service review request, as you know the importance of reviews. A birthday email is a polite and surprise way to keep the relationship. Finally, a re-engagement campaign for those not heard from hopes to bring them back to your tribe.

MailerLite, ActiveCampaign, Customer.io, MarketoEngage, Klaviyo are some to do this with.

Reaching out is also sending phone texts. Texts can and should be personalized, contain links, and more. QR code links via generators are popular too. It's all about "Attract, Engage, Delight." Multiple tools and methods do that.

> *A good marketing ROI is a ratio of 5:1 making $5 for every $1 spent.*

An ROI of 2:1 is barely profitable because other business expenses reduce that ratio closer to 1:1 or breakeven. So, what was the purpose of the campaign then? You built brand awareness and buzz, but you've lost the $$ spent on marketing/advertising unless it brought in profits.

Paid advertising is a trade between the costs of ads versus sales revenue, but email costs nothing or little except the time to compose it and send it. AI and email scripted sequences do it automatically by how a user does or doesn't respond. **They are worth the cost because they don't require much effort to create or be effective.**

Dotcoms like Constant Contact and Campaign Monitor have email templates, and others too like GetResponse or Delivra. **Check for comparisons of features and costs that suit your purpose. Make sure their process fits your goal.**

Capterra.com offers software product lists and comparisons. Their "Email Marketing Software" list shows 954 products, top picks first, with links to their websites.

Whichever product you choose, start small and cheap. Expand as contacts, sales, and funding grow. Easily export or import your email contact lists to/from another platform.

Chapter 43 Avenues of outreach

*C**hester says:* ***You'd be surprised at how accessible outlets for marketing and promotion are.*** *The online marketing world is your new millennium oyster, and it can produce pearls of great wealth.*

TV and Radio

R

It's the Age of Transition, moving to online only. FM radio, although still popular in cars, gave way to tv video in cars, Sirius XM, streaming and data feeds, and audiotapes. There are moves afoot to abolish AM radio, and CD drives are absent from newer cars. We can't keep up with change, so go with it.

That leaves television news or ads sent digitally through feeds, cable broadcasts, satellite etc. to homes, phone, email, and everywhere. **Your best bet is to finagle an interview on a tv morning show or radio, it's free. Or a podcast.**

To do that, you need to be a fad, new, popular, clever, or au currant, and have an interesting angle. Know your subject, use conversational tones when speaking to the camera or microphone (audience), and wear nice attire. TV and radio station producers will guide you or give you a script.

They are thirsty for popular new content and personalities who deliver it with enthusiasm. They are scrambling for interesting content.

Good news: TV and radio show producers are searching for good or soundbite content to fill the thousands of hours they broadcast. Offer a twist.

You can and should offer yourself as a guest speaker or presenter. You know stuff. Share it. Get the exposure. **Show benefits.** Or there are audio ads or radio ads. I've heard (on the radio) that the best times for radio were the '70s and '80s—and right now.

Check out iHeart Media for radio. They say they're #1 in digital, audio, and other media, and reach 9 out of 10 Americans every month. Check https://www.iheartmedia.com/advertising for their marketing options.

Working on radio can offer more timely and faster options to get aired. **According to Statistica, there are over 15,000 thousand AM and FM commercial stations in America.**

This article lists stations by state: https://en.wikipedia.org/wiki/Lists_of_radio_stations_in_the_United_States

They equally crave content, sponsors, and advertisers. What you need in your ad is a pleasant voice, a sales pitch, and sound. Hit listeners in 15, 20, or 30-second ad spots, or longer infomercials. Plus, there are a few thousand non-profit and educational stations. Mostly you deal with the media company first, then pick the station(s), then your airing spots. More popular spot times cost more, like daily commuting hours.

For an extensive list of radio outlets and companies, search "American media conglomerates."

Janet and I have been longtime members and listen daily to WHYY, a local National Public Radio station, but they don't "advertise" with sales pitches. They exist on contributing members, sponsors, and donations. We need more corporate and taxpayer support and sponsors of public radio.

We still listen to the radio, in cars and vehicles mostly, or we have iPods for listening to books on CD or to have phone conversations or conduct business. New cars have built-in phone systems. Like Alexa in homes, we listen to music libraries with fewer commercials.

Audio is very hot in general. CDs are disappearing as a component of new PCs, since software programs are now downloaded digitally, or not sold separately except for video games and DVD movies. New cars have "Info" centers, TVs too.

Make your radio spot:
- **Repetitive**   Memorable
- **Interesting**   Short
- **Timely**   Repetitive

Your message must be brand, brand, brand, since it's difficult in a car to pull over and write a telephone number or web address. Know the station's
- Reach in number of listeners
- Demographics
- Cost and Frequency of appearance
- Listening area or region

Podcasts

> Around 28% of Americans tune in to a podcast every week. They are offered by everyone.

Podcasts are audio only or audio and video, and production costs are extremely low. A good microphone such as a Samsung Q9U-Dynamic with Pop filter, earphones like Logitech, and a recording space with a plain background are all you need.

Recording software/ programs like Murf, Audacity, Reaper, Adobe Audio, or others have editing tools. With the external mic at your desk, create better quality digital audio recordings and files. You can "podcast" from your phone. Toktokkies do.

PowerPoint-like visuals and good graphics will hold audience interest, and above all, no lags. Silence is deadly, so keep moving. Use Zoom et al. to show YouTube etc. videos/audio. It can be live and you control the interactions, or recorded and offered over and over.

Webinars

Zoom, Jitsi, Webex, GoToMeeting, Google Meet, Butter, Tandem, Around, Bluejeans, Webex, Microsoft Teams—there are many, some free. Host a webinar, record it, and it will have a long shelf life. Intro yourself at the beginning and those joining in and take questions via chat and answer at the end.

Use PowerPoint to show points on-screen and keep eyeballs engaged, or show documents, PDFs, graphics, or photos. **Have your company name and web address on every page**

together with copyright info. Offer presentations free in return for their email address.

According to Wyzowl, 62% of marketers distribute webinars. Attract participants with helpful information and include how you or your service helps them. Sell just your service. Offer interesting and related content, or market data too, and attract larger audiences. Speak in normal conversational tones and no $10 words. Remember, just be human.

Videotape or record it and publicize the broadcast via meeting links. Offer it in your newsletter, to your email contact lists, etc. Whether a podcast, webinar, or Zoom presentation, make sure your content is:

- Relevant and Timely   Topical and Interesting
- Speaks to an audience   Has good graphics
- Has no technical glitches Starts & ends on time

Whatever you produce or share with others, who may be strangers to you, be well prepared. Have a script or outline.

Newspapers

Most printed newspapers are for local communities. Their circulation numbers matter, online too.

R

Where we get our news has changed dramatically since the internet and the iPhone. When I start my PC, Edge brings up its home screen and the day's news and weather. Home newsprint deliveries are spotty and ending. I know, since our local Times paper just cut Saturday issues.

But our weekend New York Times has a circulation of 670,000 print subscribers, and 9.41 million digital-only ones. My wife still loves both in her hands, and she reads them cover to cover. **All things digital are easier and cheaper to do, and that means creating ads too.** The NY Times must love, love, love all the digital advertisers they have now, tons more than in printed papers.

When they include online fill-ins for crossword puzzles, word jumbles, sudoku, and anagrams the transition will be complete. **Online is a boon for news outlets, not a bust. Except: competition for eyeballs and ears online is ferocious.**

For now, local papers show your best message and contact info if you operate a box store locally. Color ads are more expensive but catch the most attention. Submitted ads can be a jpeg file whether for print or digital. Online has replaced the venerable shouting newsies on Brooklyn streets.

U.S. newspaper print advertising will be around $6 billion in 2024. U.S. online advertising around $395 billion, and direct mail about $41.7 billion (2022). Email marketing is around $10 billion but is much cheaper to perform. Large outfits may use tv and radio too.

G

The first major advertising venture for Chesterfield Learning Center was paying several hundred dollars to have a blue sticky note attached to a county weekly newspaper with 50,000 subscribers. With the help of a salesperson from the paper, we designed a simple ad and offered a free introductory lesson for $400.

But only one mother of an elementary-aged student came to us with the ad, took the lesson, and she chose not to have additional lessons.

Local newspapers are community focused. Local, local, local. World, national, state, even county news is minimal. What's your market?

R

The prime benefit of print papers is that you reach thousands of local households and they have something tangible in their hands. If you are a local storefront business, then it's necessary. In my community, The Hamilton Post reaches 40,000 households and businesses, and 1/4-page color ads are cheap at $270 each per monthly edition.

If rates are low, use color print ads to achieve brand awareness or attract inquiries locally. **How you handle customers once in your store, or online, is the key to your future. You must get their cellphone number or email address. That's the golden ticket to a relationship and further sales.**

The benefit of other outlets, email, and online news or events submission systems is that you may submit to them free or pay less for an ad or blurb. Always include your web address and phone number.

Every medium has its pros and cons. Decide your audience, media, goal, and costs before advertising. ***Always have a Call to Action.***

Cold calling

R

"The best of times, the worst of times."—Tale of Two Cities
   Times are the same, yet they differ. The endless cycle of life containing cycle after cycle after cycle within it.

For sure, technology has changed for phones. Landlines are being phased out, starting in 2025. Facetime is amazing. Phones on cable, fiber, or satellite networks in homes and businesses, with cellphone roaming and Wi-Fi have been here quite a while. Texting, hash-tagging, links, QR codes, videos, emails, etc. inundate our smart cellphones now.

$25 per month per line buys all that.

But it hasn't bought me 100% privacy. I'm tired of checking phone messages and its blank, or voicemails from sales mongers or donation beggars who pine on and on until I interrupt them. **Therefore, I don't answer unknown callers. Millions of people don't. Even AARP recommends that.** That's what answering machines and voicemail are for. It's a protection against scammers, even if the number ID shown is local.

If I do pick up my landline at home or take a cellphone call from a number I don't recognize, I say nothing. About 80% of the time, it's silent and hangs up. A Robo dialer. If there is a live person, I don't confirm who I am, instead I ask, "Who's calling?" If it's legit, we speak. If not, they're phishing.

I'm ready with, "Don't call again; take me off your list."

Do not say "Yes" to an unknown caller under any circumstances. Do not hit a # key in response to their message. Scammers record that and use it to confirm your purchase or commitment to pay. Be tough since you're in business and wanting calls from potential customers. **Just be careful.**

> *The only valid phone numbers are the ones you call, someone you know, or calls you expect.*

Reputable firms will not call you. Neither Amazon, the government, your bank, and especially not Social Security or Medicare. Today, 99% of legitimate communications are by email or snail mail. **Average cold calling success rate is 2%. That's a 98% failure rate.**

Only call customers who will recognize you to offer a special, or discounts, or an invitation. When promoting your business, do not waste $$ on cold calling. We are tired, fed up, and mad at those ding-dong ringers. Even Caller ID can't tell which is fake or real. **Instead, use email to communicate.**

Email is a written record. You can check the sender's email address, or block them, or send them to trash. Or make them Spam, report them, and block them from your In-basket.

Email has that magic 44% ROI. Spend 5-10% to automate your website and emails and still receive 34% ROI.

Scammed

G

Just after my grandson was born, Ilene took a train to Pennsylvania to help my daughter-in-law with her newborn, leaving me alone in the office. In walked a middle-aged, high-energy woman with a briefcase. Debbie took out several laminated placards. Each was 8 1/2" x 17" size, folded in the middle, colorfully printed, commonly used for menus.

"While people wait for their food," she explained, "they always look for something to do."

Sure enough, on the placards were riddles, jokes, and bits of odd information, surrounded by images of business cards. I thought people would surely see our advertisement and consider using our services.

Time was short: "If you don't reserve a spot for your business card, another business will surely take your place," Debbie said.

I liked the idea we would be connecting with area restaurants, for we had an excellent rapport with a Chinese restaurant near our learning center. I called Ilene and asked her what she thought. She was not as excited as I but said that if I thought it was a good idea to go ahead.

I forked over a check for $500, expecting to see a copy of the placard in a few weeks.

Weeks passed—no placard. Ilene called Debbie's number, only to have her respond, "I'm sorry, production is delayed while I get a few more restaurants. We're on it."

More weeks passed—still no action. Ilene called some numbers on the business cards on the sample placard. Some people listed on the placard had never heard of the service; others had paid for their cards to be included, but never heard back. One company had even paid Debbie by credit card, and finally, looking through their records, realized that money had been coming out of the account for more than a year!

Frustrated, we contacted the police.

A few days later, a detective informed us that people all over Virginia were looking for Debbie. She had a mailbox at a local package and mailing service that could reveal nothing about the renter without a court order.

We had all been scammed. As a last resort, we set about laying a trap for her.

DO NOT GET PRESSURED INTO IMPULSIVE DECISIONS!

Our learning center lay in the middle of a strip mall divided into three sections, with a hamburger chain business at one end and a beauty parlor at the other. Into one of the vacant spaces a skin-care business was about to move in. Coincidentally, the police station was on the other side of it. With an officer's knowledge, we arranged a sting.

Since we knew Debbie preyed on new businesses, Ilene called her and pretended to be the owner of the new shop and asked if a meeting could take place there. We set up a time and informed the police. Since Debbie had not yet met Ilene, she stood outside waiting. I lurked around the corner with my iPad, ready to record a video that could go on "America's Somewhat Wanted."

A half hour after the appointed time, Ilene called the number Debbie had provided, only to hear, "My sister's in the hospital, we'll have to postpone." We believe she could have driven through the parking lot and become suspicious. Our one and only sting operation turned into a failure.

This experience fed our cynicism about advertising.

Phone and online scammers are super clever and brazen, and don't want to meet you in person. Always research the company first.

The #1 scam on the FTC list of top five in 2022 is Imposter Scams. #2 is Online Shopping scams, #3 Prizes, Sweepstakes, Lotteries, #4 Investments, #5 Business & Job Opportunities. Note how the loss from business imposters soared.

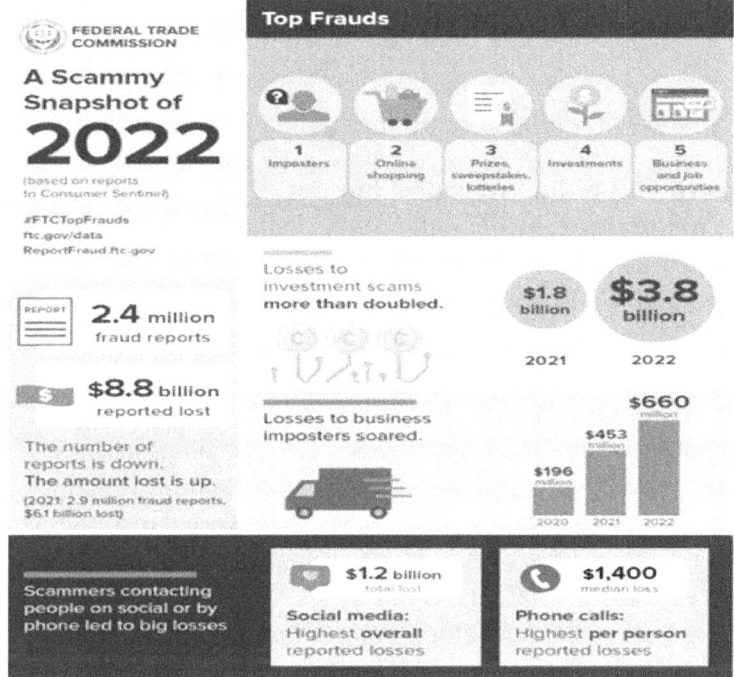

Chapter 44 Website and SEO

*C*hester says: ***Be consistent on your website, in your blog, your business profiles, social media, and marketing.***

R

Your mission is to leave enough visible breadcrumbs in this vast forest called the Internet so that anyone will follow and find you easily. And want to. You are leading them to your website, blog, business profile, social media, advertisements, sales pages, and checkout pages or links to any of them enticing enough to be clicked. SEO is about customers finding you.

   SEO is how specific keywords, items, descriptions and phases, pictures, videos etc. turn up high in internet search results. What turns up high is based on the browser's algorithm.

Always test your business name, your name, brand logo, service etc. Results vary by browser, your chosen advertiser(s), and their platforms. **Paid ads turn up the highest.**

Perfect your website

There are 1.13 billion websites, but only 200 million plus are active, maintained, or visited.
  Websites are the visible tip of the iceberg. Networking, Ethernet, and Wi-Fi power them and lie hidden underneath. Websites allow three things: instant credibility, a connection, and opportunities to build a following.
  With WordPress, Wix, or Weebly, you'll have both a host and website builder templates that make it easy for no or low cost. For less than $20-$40 per year each, lease an annual domain name URL from GoDaddy, HostGator, Web.com, Hostinger or another provider. Choose a URL extension like .net, .info, .biz, or .com for commercial, among others.
  Making yours stand out among the millions of websites is hard, but it's done every day. All website builder software has easy to use Templates to get started, then refine them and customize. Good ones improve SEO also. **Company size or name is not the only magnet. Content, ease of use, attractiveness, popularity, and security count.**

Popularity is a mystery. But one person brought their idea to market, and it caught on. Consider yourself an inventor and entrepreneur.

  Mass acceptance by hundreds first, then thousands of people, creates influence, buzz, referrals, and sales. It's a tsunami. It's a big deal to receive a silver plaque from YouTube management for having 100,000 views, or a gold one for 1 million.
  TikTok, Facebook and others give out awards too. Use them in promotion.

Search engines

R

Mozilla Firefox, Google Chrome, Microsoft Edge/Bing, DuckDuckGo, Yahoo, Ecosia are major browsers, i.e. web crawlers or search engines and offer protective searches built in. Avast, Norton, AVG, IObit and others have safe browsers too.

Search Engine Optimization is a process that optimizes a website's content and structure to improve its visibility and ranking in search engine results pages. SEO involves many techniques to master, including keyword research, on-page optimization, technical optimization, and link building in combination.

Search engines have proprietary algorithms that scour the World Wide Web in systematic ways as specified in a textual web search query by a user. To get 500,000 results is average, but as we all know, most aren't relevant. **The #1 goal of search engines is to pull up the most common answer, or the one closest to the inquiry. That is, on the first page.**

It's as if a question mark ? was at the end of every search term. **Specifics in search queries equal better results.**

Keywords bring up familiar responses of name brands or companies, new ones, articles or YouTube videos and others. They are supposed to be the top, meaningful, exact results, not iffy or circumspect, or old. They may be the most popular clicked on "answers" to searches or hardly used.

Google's search engine looks for matches in Quality, Meaning, Relevance, Useability, and Context, and uses synonyms as well.

But not all results are real. If the link looks weird you may have a compromised browser. A compromised browser usually produces old, outdated results or suspect links. For example, if you question your search engine on Windows 11, and only Windows 7 appears, something's wrong.

Google is the biggie, 8.5 billion searches per day. Go to Google Search Console, start, and register, for free analytics of your website. The U.S. Government is fighting Google because they are so dominant in the internet search space.

> *To show up in a search, be relevant.*

Numbers of hits come next. The more hits a URL or link or keyword has, the higher SEO pops it up. Rule of thumb is to appear on page 1. <u>Paid ads get top billing.</u>
For example, on sales sites like Amazon, I as an author provide each book with keywords and phrases to help my search standings. **The most common top results are company, product, service, brand names, or specific answers to specific inquiries.**

With every ad campaign, you'll choose the target audience, maybe location, income, even country, and keywords. See where you and competitors pop up in search results. **Most internet searchers won't go to page 2 or later.**

Whatever keywords you think of to draw attention to yourself, test it. Record how high the expected result appears. **When your ad campaign is in full swing, always retest. Look for improvement.**

There's no way around it. The only way to appear in top results on Internet searches is to be searched on, clicked on—a lot, or pay for it. Search engines are programmed that way, even though we all see meaningless results the more pages we scroll through. Use terms and keywords or phrases on your website and in your ads people are likely to use.

That means:
- Be memorable
- Be somewhat specific
- Be something people want, need, or desire
- Pay for ads to get top billing
- Use keywords in titles, blurbs, slogans, and copy text
- Publish quality, authoritative content, and timely
- Be mobile friendly. Most searches start there
- Add multimedia content, pictures, images etc.
- Refresh your pages
- Follow trends
- Include metadata

This HubSpot SEO information kit is helpful:
https://blog.hubspot.com/marketing/seo

Keywords and phrases are how to be found or not.

For online content, SEO is king.
The better website-builders have SEO tools and methods like Squarespace.com does: SEO, Traffic, Traffic Sources, Website, Commerce, Marketing, Scheduling, Assets, Analytics, Profiles/Subscribers. These tools allow every page of your website to be a useable link. It costs $149/yr for Basic.

Scan this article from Google, it's helpful: https://developers.google.com/search/docs/fundamentals/seo-starter-guide For your website, Google has a URL Inspection Tool to show search results for anything entered. Its link is in the article above

Make business profiles

One means of coming up high in search engine results is to have business profiles. A business profile is simple to create, easy, and cheap to populate on the Net. It may only be a few details, but it has a link to your website too.

Put up business profiles on Google Business, Microsoft Partner Center, Yelp, Bing Places, Angi and others. Update them monthly.

Search engines scour the Net, so wherever it finds your company name, your personal name, a tagline, or logline, keyword, or what's related to you, it will find it and move it higher in search results. Unless something else is higher yet, like a paid ad from a competitor, or sales of a competitor's paid product. But don't start a bidding war over that.

Business profiles get your name in multiple places. Include: web address, physical address, phone number, your name, and business hours. A map location too, if in a physical building.

Keep a list of where your business is listed on the Net. When customers come to you, ask where they heard about you. If one site or source sends many people your way, consider advertising more there.

Cookies, cookies, cookies

Delete them from your device: but leave yours on a customer's or potential customer's device.

They are a two-edged sword. Companies, advertisers, everyone wants to identify you and your preferences. Cookies help ID you, find you, and find out your preferences, which all helps advertisers and companies that advertise.

Cookies are a bit of internet server http code that do that, especially when you return to that company's or advertiser's site. Cookies let you leave a webpage and return later where you left off.

As a vendor or seller, you want to identify your contacts or those who searched and found you. Cookies do that through their Personalization Function which targets likes.

But as a user of an internet device, if you'd rather have privacy, cookies clog up your system and identify you. Every online business sends them to you. Trackers do to. They stay around until deleted. On Google they'll delete automatically as a minimum setting or you can clear them manually.

There are four types. "Strictly necessary" are just that. As a user you may want to open a screen or link and you must accept their cookie to see their page, or to logon. Or the page you want to view says "This site uses cookies." Click "No" for the other three, Functional, Analytic, and Marketing. Sometimes too your browser will pop up a small box and ask you to Allow or Block them. Block them unless you want to be remembered.

Your online customers or contacts make these choices too. **But the internet doesn't care. If cookie data isn't found it just leaves another bit of data in a new cookie.**

Everyone wants your device identity information, buying habits or preferences. Cookies give that.
  As a user you may not want or need that, but as an advertiser you do.

In your browser settings, select "clear" for browsing history, cache, cookies, and temporary images. Keep password and autofill data if comfortable with that. Use utility software like Glary Utilities, IObit Advanced System Care, CCleaner, Fortect, Norton Utilities et al. to clean cookies out. The browsers and security products also have such cleaners.

Google is testing the elimination of third-party cookies for Chrome users, around 63% of browser users. That will change the face of current practices.

Chapter 45 Social media

Chester says: *We're social beings, always have been and will be. Its big business being human.*

Even God realized Adam needed a mate. We would all like that and seldom want to live alone for long. We build a family, then a tribe, community, and nation. Now there are worldwide communities of every kind, easily accessible online.

You are trying to build a social and public family around you and your business. Social media started taking off in the mid-'90s and morphed into much more. Trace its path at https://en.wikipedia.org/wiki/Social_media

Social media is communication from one to another or groups (remember Yahoo Groups?), with most of it shown as one's views, experiences, gripes, bon mots, or self-promotion. Business loves its promotional aspects and milks it extensively.

Since 2000, **The Monetization of Everything** has gripped the Net and everything else. Facebook, with 3 billion users, started in 2004; Instagram in 2010; LinkedIn in 2003; micro-blog

Twitter in 2006 and Tumblr in 2007; Reddit in 2005; Pinterest in 2010; TikTok in 2017; Google+ launched in 2011 and ceased in 2019. There are thousands of specific ones, like Goodreads for book readers. Basically all make their $$ from advertisers.

Most are free to join as an individual. But many allow you to "attach" a business-type page under your name or form a group. And they have advertising plans and campaigns you can pay for.

LinkedIn is the outlier for companies, business related people, jobs, and sharing. Definitely join and use it.

Most, like Facebook, Instagram, LinkedIn, Pinterest, and Twitter 'X', TikTok et al., are "scrollers." Postings enter and leave your viewing screen as you scroll down through them in a never-ending stream by date and time posted.

Posts "roll off" social media feeds very quickly. It's an old-time piano roll of vignettes, photos, graphics, or words, so those looking at your feed will only see yours and what others added. New posts replace older ones. A user spends on average, 24 minutes viewing at a time, but another stat is 2.5 hours a day.

"Viewing time" is short for single posts because viewers rarely stop scrolling. On FB the average for one post is 1.7 seconds. As time passes, there are so many new posts, a specific one is impossible to find. About 57% of FB users keep themselves partially Private. About 79% don't share their data.

Email addresses aren't shown or given out in social media sites. It's near impossible to get another user's email address unless they share it in a post or through direct messaging.

Responses depend greatly on what you post: 1) information only, maybe a link, 2) an indirect link to another selling site that has your item or service, or 3) a direct link to your website's sales page and "Buy me."

Social media pages are rapid flowing no matter the platform. **Tuesdays and Thursdays 8 a.m. to noon is best to post your**

message on FB, according to a Hootsuite study. Also Tues. 2-6 pm, or Wed. 2-5 pm in general.

You specify whether posts are "Public," and anyone can see them, or "Private," for only your friends or connections. Your name, Likes, emojis, and Comments identify who you are to others, theirs to you do the same. **Those cute hearts or smiling yellow faces mean nothing in hard $$ sales but tell you if you are on the right path.**

One strategy companies and entrepreneurs use is to build up "tribes" into communities of engaged followers and get their messages and offerings to them. Joining the "tribe" is encouraged, with incentives, or a fee. The number of followers or members tells how many may use it.

Tribe members feel special. It builds hype and spreads the word like a pre-publishing book launch. Entrepreneurs give discounts and specials to their "tribe." Note though, some groups don't allow direct sales pitches or links. Social Media posts can point viewers to anything because they contain words, pictures, videos, and links. **Pictures and videos receive more attention.**

However, some stats show that 54% of FB users use it only for brand research. Instagram posts higher, at 62%. It means that a few users are more likely to choose the brand researched and found, but actual sales figures are unknown.

Only .08% engage with video posts on FB.

It's even less for link only posts, which are common on Twitter's "X." **When it comes to the effectiveness of posting on social media, it's informative, even flashy, but poor for conversions/sales unless supplemented with paid advertising.**

The "audience" for social media sites, FB, Instagram, LinkedIn, Reddit, SnapChat, WhatsApp, "X," and YouTube (although that is technically a Channel, full of visual/voice "shows"), is the Feed or Feeds, "Friends," or others.

It's a crapshoot who may see your post or ad in real-time or anytime else, much like most advertising. Sites may have ad campaign builders and decent analytics. Views are one thing, like impressions, and CTRs entirely something else.

When you advertise on social-type sites, most charge a "click-per-view" of your ad, which adds up quickly, and is

not an actual purchase of your item.** Most sites have a $$ spending cap you set per day, per campaign length.

Only gauge your ad campaigns by actual conversions and CTRs if you can. Carefully weigh your breakeven points and profits before extending campaigns. **Do your research well or get kicked in your wallet or purse teeth. They are slick money grabbers because advertising revenues pay their salaries and profits.** They give preference to paying advertisers, of course.

Your best ads will link to your sales page and a CTR. On your webpage is best; someone else's, second best. Your goal? Send traffic to your sales page and make more $$.

How it should work

"To get known, it pays to advertise." It costs to.
Retailers who host other people's and company's ads and advertisements make out like bandits. But that's how every advertiser works to rake in profits. **They provide a large ready-made user base or media platform you can't compete with.** You pay them to show your ad, in whatever shape or form you or someone makes for you.

Social media is "free," to join and use unless you sign up for 'X' Blue. Post almost anything on your feed and respond to others' feeds. If you advertise on them, you pay the host, whether FB, Reddit, or whoever, **but they may not show you when or where your ad appears, or how often, and you must trust their method of counting.**

At least with a print newspaper I'll see my ad on page 15. If online and you pay a per-click charge for it, they show you how many viewers clicked it, and when. But because they can't link to your sales page, they can't tell how many bought it.

That's how advertising really works. A pretty poor investment without direct evidence of your success or profit. Successful advertising means matching views with increased

sales. CTRs. Therefore, do not pay for a "click per view" campaign. It's a waste of your money unless it is a click on your Buy link, is followed through with buyer payment, and can be tracked and reported.

Selling direct B2C is the most profitable, it's a large audience. But not always practical. There are pitfalls to direct product sales. You must stock inventory, collect sales taxes, remit them, and mail or deliver the product. For services, however, it's easy, just work from an initial inquiry. Then agree on terms, sign an agreement online, do the job and receive payment.

If your item or service offering is on a seller's site like Amazon, or Shopify for example, you pay them a fee to host you and to perform the Merchant Services for you. They show you your CTRs and daily sales.

Follow what is available or used for your specific industry. Adopt methods that fit your business needs. Look at case studies that fit you.

Summary on social media

Social media gives you thousands of opportunities to share and build a fan base. Hundreds of ways are free, like joining and posting to like-minded groups. Use them as a foundation.

Some social media sites/advertisers are building technical ways to match your ad to actual sales, say from your website, an interface, like Squarespace does. In Squarespace Basic, or others, each page has its own URL. That's best.

Bottom line: whomever you build your website with or advertise with, it's best to use those who link to your actual sales and show it to you. **To hell with "how many viewers clicked." Show me the money.**

A word about social media ad campaigns: Each vendor/ site has their own schemes. On FB for example, the first thing you do is specify the objective of your campaign. That's:

Awareness	**Traffic**	**Engagement**
Leads	**App promotion**	**Sales**

Those six areas will be where you spend your ad dollars. They are intricately related, and you can get really specific, like city. The best bet is to combine their objectives into your ads for the optimum results you want. You need to know how to market and make sales. Check information from Salesforce.com, HubSpot.com, or learn social media marketing from WordStream.com.

Specific tools help reach potential customers and hook them. Too many with specific schemes to mention. MailerLite, and Convert kit work for emailing newsletters, for example. **Check your vendor's tutorials/articles/blogs, and support on how your chosen platform(s) work and how to set them up.** YouTube has great stuff also.

Chapter 46 Merchant Services

Chester says: *Merchant services are synonymous with banking services for buying and selling things or services.*

Merchant services are payment-related business support services and equipment, whether physical or digital. Its electronic purchases and app purchases, also called Purchase-to-pay or P2P, procure-to-pay, eProcurement, or req-to-cheque. The purchase-to-pay process is automated, saves costs, and reduces risk.

Merchant Services (MS) handle Point of Sale (POS) payments, deposit funds into seller's bank accounts, credit cards, or cyber-wallet via Electronic Funds Transfer (EFT).

R

Ecommerce provides a selling function for you to sign up for and receive and deposit customers' funds into your account for a percentage and transaction fee.

With ecommerce you create your items or services and prices, use a company's templates, list them on their site on your "store shelf," link your bank account, and these sites display your items/prices and automate the customer's buying process.

When someone buys your item(s), the MS company processes the transaction, takes their cut, then transfers your cut to you. Thousands of stores, sites, and vendors do it because it increases the number of items on their site available for sale and means more profits. **The MS function handles purchases, taxes, and payments.**

Online sellers deposit your proceeds into your bank account after they take their cut. Or pay more to get your funds out the same day, like with PayPal. **Merchant service companies or sales sites/ companies remit immediately or monthly. Be wary if they hold your $$ too long.**

How you use them relates to your sales methods, i.e. Direct or Indirect Sales. If selling from your website directly, check out the following providers: Helcim, Stripe, Payment Depot, Square, U.S. Bank, Dharma, Quickbooks (Intuit) or others. Check comparisons on NerdWallet.com.

Merchant Servicers charge a percentage and per transaction fee. Compare terms and fees.

FinTech Firms

With Financial Technology firm systems and apps, you can sell items or services directly from your website, social media, in person, from a store, sitting in your car from your phone, on land or sea, even on a plane. It's electronic and digital.

These servicers work on your PC or smartphone via Electronic Funds Transfer (EFT), from your website or almost anywhere. They work with a credit card or bank account you set as a preferred way to purchase or pay. Stick with well-known, stable providers like PayPal, Apple Wallet or Google Pay, et al.

When you sell items, they take a percentage and per transaction fee based on dollar amounts they handle. A client may transfer $100 to your PayPal business account, but after PayPal's fees, you'll receive around $95.71. It's a necessity, but **Fin Tech companies have a +/ 2% higher fee than a credit card.**

It's the cost of doing business to you for convenience, and buyers expect you to have one of these services. Customers can use a credit card online or a phone app to pay you, or you can pay vendors/others the same way. Some, like Square, have a Tap to Pay phone app, which takes a physical or keyed in credit card in person.

Only use established, secure services that invoice, pay, or receive payments. Track transactions via EFT.

With FinTech firms, all you really need is an email address or moniker to bill someone or receive a transferred payment. Also use name and location as a best practice. In PayPal, you include a note about what it is for. With Square, you issue canned or customized invoices or requests.

Whichever you use, Merchant Services or FinTech, be sure to transfer or deposit your received payments from them directly into your bank account and ledger if they don't automatically do it.

Print summaries of these transactions or and reconcile them with your monthly bank statements. Each firm has their own agreement and Terms of Use, area of expertise, methods, dashboards, availability, and fee structure, so check carefully.

If you sell directly or transfer $$, use Stripe.com, Square.com, Helcim, PaySafe, PayPal, Google Pay, MerchantOne, Apple Pay, or ProMerchant etc.

Collecting sales taxes

R

The great benefit about seller sites like Amazon.com and Google Play where my books are sold, is that they collect sales tax too. That makes it extremely easy. For every book of mine sold online, the customer is charged the NJ sales tax at the point-of-sale, since NJ is my nexus. It's transparent, meaning it's added to every sale price automatically.

The other great thing about this embedded processing function is that it's built into the transaction fee structure merchants charge all clients/customers, and not separate. **Otherwise, as the seller, you must collect and remit sales taxes to your nexus state.**

The rule is: if the marketplace doesn't do this for you, then you pay federal or state taxes because you should've legally collected them. Some sale sites are just go-betweens, where you list your item or service and they take a cut when it sells, but they don't process taxes. For example, Craig's List, Angi, and Freelancer.

In selling your services or whatever online, eCommerce sites comply based on their proprietary business model, like Facebook Marketplace, the Apple Store, Shopify, Etsy, Amazon, and most shopping sites. Google has Buy on Google, Google Play, and Google Store, and there are more places to sell on tons of sites. You can sell products or some services on Amazon through their Seller Central Account.

Chapter 47 Expand your influence

Chester says: *Influencers cheer others on, or projects, or causes. They sing praises. If you cheer them on, they sing louder.*

Decades ago, there circulated a list of 20 items titled, "The Effectiveness of Sales Methods." It ranked them. They were radio, tv, email, flyers, business cards, snail mail etc.

> At the top of the list was Word of mouth. In our online world, direct interaction is like word of mouth.

You know this yourself. If you need a plumber, a new appliance, a new tv or what neighborhood with a good school to send your kids to, you ask friends and relatives. You know them, trust them, and value their opinions. You are more likely to contact whomever they recommend.

If you personally hear their kudos of someone or something, you're more attracted. In 2023, this is the same as online product and service reviews. They are critical to success.

Coddle influencers

> *If an influencer likes and trusts you, they influence others. Reviewers are influencers.*

Influencers make or break you. And everyone influences someone or something, even huge masses. Influencers get the word out, start fads, and promote you, because they like or admire you and what you've done. And when they trash you, right or wrong, fix it or defend it.

A few words from Charli D'amelio on TikTok can make you go viral, especially since he has 148 million followers. That's power. Also, it's why endorsements have always been used to sell products. Today, reviews are critical.

> *Participate in like-minded groups. Join on social media and post once in a while. Develop discussions and conversations that elevate not denigrate. Stay in touch.*

Even if someone doesn't buy from you, they are an influencer. Everyone you meet or speak to is an influencer. Those who view your website, ads, products, or use your services, are all influencers. Those who read your social media posts, blogs, newsletter, or podcasts are influencers.

That's why, "Always be nice. You never know who's watching." More than that, provide something useful. Your rep means a lot here.

R

In 2010-2011, I had been attending weekly writing critique sessions with a group of 14 writers. I had learned a lot, all good stuff. I wanted to continue, but I thought, maybe I can start a group closer to where I live?

I went on my local Hamilton Twp. Library website, found the Director's email, and sent him a proposal:

"Dear Director Conwell,

"My name is Rodney Richards. I'm a longtime Hamilton resident, writer, and published author, retired from the State of NJ. I currently attend writing critique sessions at the Lawrence Library and wonder if we could start them at the Hamilton Library? These free sessions would be open to the public. We'd share our writing, offer positive feedback, help improve and encourage each other, and promote literacy and better writing.

"We would need a small room, and a time convenient to the library's schedule. I would facilitate. Is this possible?

"Sincerely and thank you for your consideration,

"Rodney Richards"

Within a day, he responded, "Absolutely!"

Lesson learned: Ask. If you get a "No" try something else or tweak your goal. Compromise is not a dirty word like it is for some in Washington.

We started Monday afternoon writing and critique sessions shortly thereafter. Six weeks in, eight local folks were attending. By 2013, it was fifteen. We grew to be a family, mutually promoting each other, and growing. I had a new networking group!

Later, I planned, coordinated, and presented an Author's Night at the Library using their short Bios in PowerPoint. They invited friends and family. Free publicity!

Best, our library room was free. My only expense was Staples copies of Craft Chat handouts and/or a poem or story excerpt I'd written to share with attendees. It was win-win.

Reach out. Start a group and meet or pull together like-minded people. Search out those with similar interests. Offer a service and knowledge.

Keep costs low by doing it on social media.
Look at the thousands of groups doing this.

Now do things like this free on the Net. Start a Zoom class or program, newsletter or email streams, and never leave your home. **Ask for an opportunity or make one.**

There're at least five objectives: 1. hope they like you, 2. improve, 3. sharpen your offerings, 4. sell products and services, and 5. build relationships.

Within 2 years of starting my "writing club," I had 350 email writing contacts, Instagram followers, 100's of LinkedIn contacts, 1,000 Facebook Friends, and 1,000 Google Contacts. **I knew my target audience—writers of every kind who wanted editing or publishing help. I saved time and $$ by not blasting strangers.**

The best salesperson for my books is my 95-year-old mother. Since my first memoir, she's bought my books and gives them to friends and acquaintances. They in turn bought books and gave some away too.

With automation tools, it's never been easier for solopreneurs, entrepreneurs, even big companies, to email out newsletters and attract eyeballs and followers. It's even easier to grow digital contacts with Instagram, LinkedIn, YouTube, TikTok, Facebook, Quora, Reddit and others. Personalize those connections with stories, posts, emails and more. **Use hashtags # to reach larger audiences.**

As a business owner, you are always reaching out.

Continue learning. Build on your expertise, share it, grow followers, and attract new clients.

Reach public influencers

G

Wanting to become known to the county and school district, we brainstormed ways to get our learning center name distributed at school venues. This meant getting permission. Within fifteen minutes' drive of our center were four high schools, as many middle schools, and several elementary schools.

We met with a county school-business liaison and showed them our brochures were already in use. One brochure was approved, but with the stipulation that it be left in guidance offices in case parents or students asked for tutoring help. A photocopy of our brochure was stamped by an official, permitting us to visit the schools and speak with the counselors, or more often, the principals.

They readily accepted our approved brochures, but said, "Our counselors cannot, in fairness, promote or recommend your services over other agencies." This dashed our plans.

We noted that a competitor—a national franchise—had its name and logo on tissue boxes in the guidance offices, but we realized no office would have competing tissue boxes, so we avoided that advertising dead end.

Public or educational institutions must stay neutral. However, they may accept beneficial knowledge, literacy, or social service-based programs and activities.
   And always… donations.

Every business wants to be recognized and worthwhile, even a valuable and beloved entity. It ensures longevity, loyal customers, and a good reputation. Once you have a modicum of respect and recognition, that can be leveraged 100s of ways.

It's why you see "Est. 1990" or whatever year it was on marketing materials from thousands of businesses. It proves they are doing something right, and everyone wants to be on that bandwagon.

Be determined and patient. Build upon each little success or achievement. Publicize them, share them, invite others in.

The greatest hope we hold for the businesses we frequent is this: "That they remain in business." Just like doctors who are younger than you, be glad they'll outlive you and always be there when you need them. And we need more good doctors. There's plenty of room for good businesses.

Time is a friend… or enemy

Against prevailing wisdom, know this: Time is your friend, especially as you build, build, build the business. It takes time to do anything in this contingent world, as we know. Rushing causes poor planning, inadequate preparation, and mistakes. There's "a time to hold 'em, and a time to fold 'em" in Texas and everywhere.

There's one of three ways you started your business: 1. you rushed in all gung-ho and excited, which is fine, or 2. laid the groundwork to still be around at least the first three years, or 3. were wise enough to do both.

There's no substitute for good planning, preparation, and organization. Even passion can falter. Do them well and thrive.

Chapter 48 Network and affiliate

Chester says: *Networking groups can make new and beneficial connections. Decide if they are worth your time and money.*

G

We were in our learning center location only a few weeks when an elderly gentleman dropped in asking whether we had yet joined any networking groups. Ilene found him easy to talk to, for he, too, had lived in New York City and been a Yankee fan. He introduced us to Business Networking International, known as BNI. They invited us to a meeting in Richmond the following week, so I drove over one early morning to see what they were about.

Twenty people attended, each from a distinct line of business, like one plumber, one electrician, one beautician, etc. The idea was that in each person's daily business and private life, he or she would also promote the use of the services of other members of the group. **After the welcome and overview, the purpose was made clear: acquire new customers and make money from referrals.**

Financial statements of the group followed, then everyone passed around business cards. One of the officers gave an educational moment or words of wisdom, usually taken from the international website. Individuals took a minute to introduce themselves, explain the nature of their business, and inform everyone about whom they sought to make more contact with.

One said, "Hi, I'm Joe, of Joe's Quality Landscaping, and I'm looking for an introduction to grounds managers of area developments." Others in the group responded with ideas about people they knew who might help him.

Attend free Introductory Meetings to find out if it's a good fit for your business. But organized networking groups charge member fees.
  Weigh costs against referrals received.

In addition, at weekly meetings, one member had ten minutes to inform the group of details about his or her profession. Weekly meetings began 7:30 a.m. sharp for socializing.

Members who could not attend were expected to send a substitute or designate another member.

Near the end of the gathering, members passed out leads, or names of prospective customers written on a small triplicate form. One piece would go to the person to whom business was referred, the referring member would keep a copy, and another copy would go into a bowl. Similar forms would be for "closed business," which meant a member publicly thanked a fellow member for a contract garnered through their referral. Another common practice was for the day's presenter to supply a gift card granted to the person whose slip was pulled at random from the bowl.

During one meeting, I presented a graph showing the dollars we had squandered in advertising our first year. It was partly the reason BNI sounded like it had sales potential for us. The concept of it appealed to me, but I favored joining a nearer group, so I found a BNI chapter that met in a conference room of a car dealership ten minutes from home.

Both Ilene and I visited and saw the potential for making back our $450 membership and initiation fee many times over. We stayed with them for two years but never got one referral from any of the eighteen members!

LeTip International is also a widely used and well-organized, similar networking group with hundreds of chapters and costs about $400 per year.

These groups work for many but be leery of them. ***Weigh the annual membership fee against tangible results.*** *If you are not gaining helpful business knowledge or referrals, do not renew.*

However, to be fair, our business benefited monetarily from the needs of some BNI members themselves, their children, or grandchildren who attended our learning center.

We ourselves used the services of several of the members. One BNI member owned an independent insurance company, and by switching to her, we saved $2,000 a year. We also hired a CPA from the group who could explain to Ilene the intricacies of QuickBooks that we used for our business accounting.

We also hired an air conditioning technician to clean our filters at home and help stop a horrible whistling noise. Another member, a landscaper, installed an irrigation system in our backyard, and I used the services of a member of an attorney's office for advice about an old claim, which he gave me gratis.

The most effective way to advance is still one-to-one contact through positive word of mouth, and personal recommendations. Leave reviews.

For the first time, Ilene and I hooked up with a financial planner who helped us make sense of our personal finances, including my forthcoming social security benefits and retirement plans. Ilene also got her hair cut and styled by a member who ran a beauty spa.

Within two years of our having joined the group, members started leaving, petty bickering occurred, and a core group shared among themselves and no one else. By then, no more members or students from group members used our services. We still hadn't received outside referrals, nor had we been successful in referring others.

Don't be stubborn and stay on too long or be optimistic in these groups. Don't believe you'll be guaranteed business.

We wised up and transferred to the Hull Street Association a mile closer to our home. We had difficulty but transferred our membership for the rest of our third year without having to pay the full fee. In this new group, after several months, our only connection was with the professional printer, although we gave our personal taxes to the accountant in the group and got to use a moving truck for free from one of the men.

Seek opportunities to expand your contacts. Get comfortable with diversity. People come in all shapes, colors, beliefs, and backgrounds.

Unlike Ilene, I enjoyed making new acquaintances in my role as director of the learning center, for in my personal life I kept to myself. The Hull Street Association (HSBA) was more formal, with its meetings held monthly. Most members attended in business attire and meetings were brainstorming sessions about how we could help each other succeed. Members also made presentations. The meetings provided me, and most other people there, with renewed energy and high hopes of increasing income.

Diehards, we paid annual dues and remained in the HSBA group for two years, but, again, found our investments in time and money did not yield additional business.

Promotional groups are only effective if their members offer your business card to customers.

In defense of networking groups, it depends on the local group you're in. If its members promote you well, it may be a win-win. **The only way to tell is if you recoup annual membership fees through referrals.** Ilene and I visited other groups with high expectations, but none benefited us. Twice we started our own groups, but neither got off the ground.

Upon reflection, a fledgling business like ours needed to explore what other local businesses existed in the area, what the community was like and how it ran, and to hear their anecdotes about what worked and what didn't.

Major takeaways included:
- the importance of repeat customers,

- whether to offer sales or discounts,
- the extent to which advertising media, and what types, were effective.

It was valuable information, but we got no direct referrals or sales. Therefore, paying high membership fees annually wasn't worth it to our bottom line, and we left. Like visiting the businesses in our strip mall, in this case, personal contact, not referrals, worked best.

We finally escaped the sunk cost fallacy.

Affiliations are good, but…

Chester says: ***Before becoming a member of an organization, or affiliated with one, weigh the cost of joining in terms of dollars, time, and benefits.***

G

Despite our general failure to make money from "getting our name out there" through networking groups, Ilene and I still thought about the value of becoming associated with other groups. The obvious one to belong to was CHAMPS, *Chamber Helping Achieve Meaningful Partnerships in Schools*. Their purpose was supporting the county schools and fostering a strong relationship between county chamber businesses and the public education system.

We attended several meetings and volunteered to make presentations at the schools. Expecting exposure will lead to students coming to us for tutoring. They didn't take us up on it, but we continued because we felt we should make a total commitment to educational ventures, unlike the managers of the national tutoring chains. We felt our reputation was paramount.

We stopped attending because they held the meetings during prime tutoring time, and we felt they gave the awards to schools that did little to deserve them.

> ***Seek free association and/or affiliation with like-minded groups.*** *Offer what you can, or volunteer. Get to know people.*

Similarly, we represented our business at the county Chamber of Commerce and enjoyed seeing people whom we knew, and we made new acquaintances. The meetings were held at a country club, with spinoff meetings on occasional Saturdays.

The sessions were quite popular, with over 200 people in attendance enjoying a catered lunch. I walked around and met people, and at the dinner tables we introduced ourselves, explained our businesses and swapped business cards.

Another group we joined, at inflated cost, was the Better Business Bureau.

> *The BBB is a business accreditation organization, which maintains business standards.*

We thought people seeking tutors would naturally wonder what our rating was, so we joined and hoped for a good rating. The $800 fee was steep, but at least we got a sticker to place on our window. We paid for a second year, but not the third, even though we had heard a rumor that if a company didn't remain a member, they would downgrade it a letter or two. However, even after having stopped paying dues for four years, we were pleased we still maintained an A+ ranking.

Credentials are best

R

Business owners, excited about potential, don't always choose the best fit for themselves right off the bat. I wasn't worried I didn't have formal accreditations or networking groups or

affiliations when starting RREnergy & IT Consulting back in 2009. I had proven experience and was a member of AEE, the Association of Energy Engineers, and had earned a certificate in purchasing energy. Plus, I thought I had ready-made clients.
Wrong.
But like George's experience networking groups, you must have personal credibility, critical in a services business. Personal credibility comes from training and experience, and I was selling, well, myself. Barely a high school graduate.

I had 44 nighttime college credits and a 3.9 GPA, years of state experience, an honest reputation, good writing skills, and I was well known. But I wasn't a salesperson. I knew how to buy IT stuff and millions of kilowatt hours of electricity and therms of gas, but that wasn't what state facility managers needed then.

They needed to save $$ or lower facility utility bills, not spend $$ to upgrade or switch out outdated equipment.

Chester says: You will only succeed if you give people what they need to succeed. Close won't do it. People bend backwards to save $$—not spend it.

As a writer with new goals starting with ABLiA Media in 2012, writing was a better fit for my skill set. I loved writing. For the Treasury Department I had written dozens of complex RFP's and bids. Other writers now wanted my writing critiques and tips, even signed contracts with me to edit their manuscripts. They trusted me; I respected them. Once I converted my skills to prose and poetry, it was paying off.

My potential customer base was thousands of writers.

Like a Bio, list your education and experience, awards, achievements, and accomplishments.
List companies or entities served.

For RR Energy I had the credentials, but timing wasn't right. Reflection confirmed four planets had to align just right, and for ABLiA Media, they worked seamlessly:

> The Right Time +
> The Right Credentials +
> The Right Message +
> The Right Audience
> = Connections and Sales

Draw up profiles of potential customers. What do they want or need? How can you provide it? Brainstorm where to find them. Be systematic.

Chapter 49 Carting away our money

Chester says: ***Ask, "How did you hear of us?"***

G

After just a few months of tutoring operations, a man came into the learning center with a great idea: We should advertise our new business on grocery carts. We thought, "Everyone goes to the grocery store in town."

He showed us photos of advertisements on the front of carts and inside the basket near the handle, where parents place their toddlers or small items. The ads would go on one out of every six carts at a local Martin's grocery store that averaged 20,000 shoppers a week.

He volunteered to help us construct the color ad and promised to have the carts ready within a month of our approval. The ads would be a bit larger than a license plate.

Having become a little wiser about how to spend our advertising dollars, we first visited the store and noted that as the man had mentioned, a local dance studio had its plates on carts, so we figured people would see ours and think about our signs' message too.

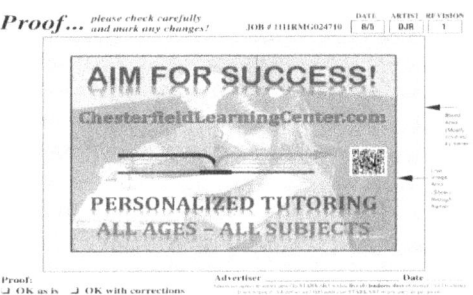

We had heard and read repeatedly that someone needs to see and hear an advertising message at least seven times before the ad becomes effective.

We returned to the office and informed him a few days later we would go ahead. We developed what we thought was the ideal ad, a nearly transparent background photo of our standard photo of me tutoring a student with our company name and telephone number on the plate. Within two weeks, the agent gave us a miniature shopping cart with a placard on it.

Do the math

We did the math: To pay for the $800 cost for advertising on our Learning Center sign on the front of the grocery carts, we only needed to enroll two SAT or ACT students to contract for twenty-four lessons. We eagerly expected the ads' appearance, going to the store every week and examining the carts.

After the deadline for the ads to be placed onto the carts had passed, we called the company, only to learn that the plates had been placed onto carts in a Martin's store several miles beyond the store close to us.

This was totally worthless. For up to that time, nobody would travel more than a few miles to use our services. Finally, after three months, the plates were installed at the correct store location and left on the carts for several months.

As a matter of curiosity, one day I boldly approached several random shoppers in the store who were using carts with our plates on them. I asked if they had noticed our ad, but the response was the same, "Oh, I never pay attention to those."

Ads are like air to most people—they don't see them or pay attention. They only see it when looking for what they want or need.

Back at the learning center, we inserted a line on student information sheets that asked, "How did you hear of us?" No responses mentioned carts, but we figured it would take a while for the ads to be effective. We were so naively trusting in the theory's viability that signed on with another firm. They placed our plates onto several hundred carts in a local Kroger's grocery store, where purportedly 27,000 people shopped each week.

After several years, not one person had indicated he or she came to us because of our advertisements on a grocery cart. We did end up with great-looking ad copy—and a cute miniature cart.

For a local business, signs and physical ads, billboards etc. give your business a familiar ring. That is the first step toward community trust. But it's a two-step process.
   Ads must pay for themselves in conversions to purchase, and some are impossible to track.

Chapter 50 Direct and indirect marketing

Chester says: *Direct marketing is selling products or services directly to the public rather than through retailers or an intermediary.*

G

Another marketing venture of our Corp involved summer camps. This did not mean going into a wilderness area with a cedar lake and counselors; rather, "summer camps" loosely meant organized activities to amuse children or teaching them arts and crafts, for example.

While our county offered summer school, it was well known that children in large groups generally learn little, so we offered a combination of academic and nonacademic programs. We developed a trifold brochure and distributed copies to all our students and parents.

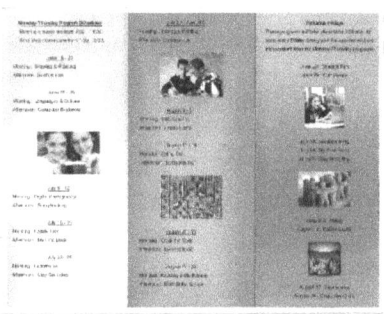

To maximize profits, Ilene and I offered weeklong programs that we could present. Some summers we succeeded than others. Our courses included typing, sewing, math, science, and others. Our reading specialist ran boy and girl book clubs, too.

A total fiasco was matching merit badges for all levels of scouting for all sexes with mini courses Ilene and I were prepared to offer. Despite offering courses to local scout troops, no students signed up.

In retrospect, I was motivated by my experience of having earned fifty-four merits as a Boy Scout and I had hoped Ilene's as a Girl Scout leader would have been used.

Direct marketing is direct to a potential customer, such as mail, email, messaging or telemarketing.

G

Over the next two years, we returned to delivering flyers ourselves and using another delivery service, but with few positive results. We figured people threw out the flyers as most of us do, were not excited about the message, or did not need a tutor. By the time we finally gave up on the idea of flyers, we had covered thousands of households within five miles. We experimented with delivering them only to homes that had a basketball hoop in the driveway, to ensure at least one child lived there.

The poor response did not merit the cost of producing flyers and our time or cost spent hand-delivering them. It meant other means of advertising our business had to be found to yield better results.

Social media marketing is direct to someone's feed through messaging or posting. Your message can be addressed individually or en masse. People respond better to direct person-to-person contact, so address them by name. Automated tools do that.

R

Direct selling was when I knocked on doors, talked to people, and sold them magazine subscriptions for my first summer job in 1965. **Your website's sales page is considered direct in online terms when it includes a "Buy me" link, despite appearing indirect.** Mainly because with one click payment is made and your bank account grows. You can collect email addresses and payment data too.

But you must also collect sales tax and make delivery when selling directly. For example, if I sold directly from my website for my books, I'd have to collect buyer information and process the credit card. I'd have to package any print book sold, address it, and pay USPS $3.92 or UPS $4.99 to ship it. That's a lot of work with less reward, higher costs, and longer processing time.

If my print book or eBook is sold indirectly, on Amazon, Google Play, Book Baby, Smashwords, or Digital2Digital, the "Buy me" link is on their website, and they take the order and payment, deliver my eBook digitally, and pay me royalties after their cut.

My editing and publishing services, on the other hand are indirect because they require more steps. I contract for them when someone contacts me, and we sign an agreement. I handle all details and payments using PayPal, easy-peasy.

A great deal hinges on what you are selling, where, and how. That also means how you market it. Sit down now if you haven't fully planned this out and do it. Step by tedious step, inch by inch, process by process. Weigh the costs and trade-offs. Weigh advertising costs and fees charged by other sellers. Weigh the costs to do it yourself.

Choose providers and tools based on your method of selling focused on what you offer <u>and the quickest access to it</u>. **One size won't fit all, even though your ads or sales blurbs can. "The medium is the message, but the messenger conveys the product or service."**

Indirect marketing

Indirect marketing requires an extra step for you to reach a potential customer. Most often what you or a retailer shows points to your website, phone#, product, or service. Then the actual contact begins.

Bill Gates said, **"Content is king,"** in an essay on the Microsoft website in January 1996. He effectively said he expected much of the real money in a new hooked up world will be on the internet, just as it was in broadcasting radio, then tv.

He was correct in his prediction.

Content is anywhere you see it or find it. Ads, text, images, videos, signs, webinars, podcasts, newsletters, books, blogs, website pages, social media, PR, billboards, tv, radio, books, billboards, magazines, newspapers and more.

You have content on your website and content on seller's sites that are selling your products or services for you and remitting you payment. Everything you produce should have keywords or keywords and phrases embedded in it that drive traffic to you or put you higher in search results. AI and SEO helps with that.

When selling indirectly from another's store or site, you can pay them to advertise more for you, rather than just being on some long list of available things.

Regardless how, in any kind of marketing, go after customers, reviewers, and influencers; court them. Use co-authors for your blogs or guest bloggers. Or co-presenters for podcasts and webinars. Always give their name and a little background. **People love to see their own name.** They will respond better and promote themselves and you by affiliation.

That includes sponsors, co-sponsors, and affiliations. **Affiliate with like-minded groups or complementary businesses.** Help them and they will help you; maybe even pay you.

Seek and follow up on referrals. Have a Loyalty or Rewards Program or a small bonus for using you, or a discount.

Get reviews, then post them, advertise them, and share them, especially if someone or from some company or organization that uses your products or services. **Just ask! Show favorable reviews on your website, share them on social media, and use them in marketing materials. They are gold.**

Shoppers check reviews before buying. Look at Amazon, Walmart, and any reputable online sales site, and you'll find reviews. You must get them. If not, or review numbers are low, it's a red flag.

QR Coding

A QR code on a business card or any type of marketing material is popular, since over 83% of the world's people have smartphones.

Places use QR codes to order from or reach their website, even for picking up food delivery and alerting the establishment. They are on apps, mailed ads, and your TV screen too.

Download Google's Authenticator to your smartphone for a free QR Reader. Use a QR code generator for free or a few bucks a month if you intend to use them for selling or to reach you, your website, or any URL. Businesses use them too as payment apps, and almost every store has a laser scanner to read them.

Know and serve your community

R

My township has 90,000 people. We bought a house here in 1979. Well, the mortgage company did, and I learned new skills to fix it up. Early on though, I made time to volunteer. **The best reasons to volunteer are to be of service, change what goes on, get to meet and know people, and hear local news.**

Causes, other businesses, and organizations need volunteers. Pick one. In 1984 my wife Janet co-founded the Friends of the Hamilton Library, so we're longtime members. Also, for 24 years, I was a trained volunteer municipal court mediator. I was also on our town's Environmental Advisory Commission.

At meetings, sessions, and events, I met tons of folks, heard stories, and became familiar with every neighborhood. I learned local news, and these created opportunities to share my talents, business, and published books. I met and talked to town officials. I made sales, contacts, and influencers.

Businesses with boards and committees need members too.

Volunteer locally. Join a board or commission. Get to meet people and learn about your town. It builds respect and reputation and gets your name known.

I placed my photo and a line about my business on every email I sent out as part of my automatic signature. **Hundreds of people knew a little about me, what I did, and how to reach me. Do likewise.** Make friends and fans. How do you think any politician does it? They start with the School Board and work up.

Localities, schools, counties, state governments and service orgs want reasonable citizens for all sorts of volunteer posts. It's an incredible way to build credibility and become known.

R

Become known online

There are privacy concerns and rightly so, online, and off.

Online in a public venue or feed, I would never post tirades, rants, foul stuff, my children's or grandkids photos, or the times we expected to be away from home. Only share events and pictures <u>after</u> getting back from vacation. Of course, don't share compromising photos or texts, or hate speech or violence.

I promote peace and unity among people and society as part of my Baha'i religious beliefs, but it's more than that. **It just makes common sense not to stir up things—they're stirred up enough.** I wrote and published two volumes of essays on world problems and solutions. Taking political sides is just too divisive. That doesn't mean I'm silent.

It still leaves vast opportunities to share views rationally.

Share, share, share. Be friendly, informative, and positive. Support others who share what you like.

Get your name, your face, and your brand out there.
Use wisdom. Become known for:
- Stability, longevity, loyalty, honesty, and fairness
- Flexibility and fun!

Chapter 51 Venue Ventures

C hester says: *If you represent your business at a venue, talk to everyone present, even those representing other businesses.*

Indoor venues

G

We had our storefront Learning Center front and center, open to the public during regular weekly hours. Those who came into our strip mall saw us and knew we were there, and we knew we had to get the word out wider than that. There's an old saying: "Cast one line and hook and you may catch one fish. Cast a net and catch a dozen."

Since our tutoring services were provided inside the center, we needed customers, parents, students, and referrals. **But sometimes, we did not have to seek places to advertise our goods or services; people and opportunities came to us.**

Such was the case with back-to-school events, camp programs, and charitable events in our community. Having already been connected to the school district to obtain permission to distribute our brochures, we were contacted by a liaison to consider setting up a table at an indoor Teacher Fair at the end of August, three months after we opened.

We readily accepted the offer, for about 300 teachers from various high schools would attend, where other vendors would also be present. We purchased a six-foot folding table, two folding chairs, and nifty envelope openers and packets of sticky pads with our logo on them. Further, we ordered a vinyl banner to attach to the table. Our total investment was $200, which we had already made from having tutored a calculus student.

Invest and reinvest. Put some earnings or profits back into the business for growth and expansion.

Reinvest—that was the idea—although by that time we had already taken out $5,000 from our home equity account for business expenses, not counting $2600 for rent and utilities for the fourth month of operation.

Ilene stayed at the office the day I went to the high school and set up. I was pleased to be at the far end of the cafeteria, where anyone entering could easily see my new banner with its bright red letters emblazoned upon a white background. I was one of twenty vendors, and I realized that since we each paid $50 for the privilege, the district made about a thousand dollars, which I figured more than paid for the giveaways it was donating to the visiting teachers. At our table, we also donated three VISA gift cards, $25, $20, and $15, for a raffle.

Gift card prizes for filling a survey, raffles, something of value for free, even information, are cheap ways to gather name and email addresses.

Of the hundreds of teachers at the Fair, fifty visited our table, who simply scooped up our giveaways and walked to the next vendor or else inquired whether I had any openings for tutors.

I recall an inane phrase from Captain Kangaroo: "Pickin' up paw-paws, put 'em in your pocket."

Any kind of Giveaway <u>may</u> create brand awareness and indirectly result in a referral or sale. "May" is a hope, not a guarantee. Everyone takes free stuff.

One item we gave away was a letter opener with our name and logo. We also had four different mood pencils that changed color from the warmth of a writer's hand. I left the event hoping eventually we would gain some students, but at least we "got our name out there."

"A rose is a rose is a rose," wrote Gertrude Stein. "Cost is a cost is a cost," applies to most business undertakings. Even "free" costs someone something.

We didn't receive any students from our investment in the event, but at least we now had a banner to display at future ones, and a portable table and chairs.

If you are a community-based business, visibility brings awareness and credibility. You can meet people and gather info. Online faces are invisible.

R

A good friend, Frank Yazhari, owns FYConsulting, an S-Corp. He and I collaborated on a booth display at the NJ League of Municipalities Annual Exhibition and Conference in Atlantic City, at the huge Convention Center. This when I was still RREnergy. It cost me $500 for our shared table in an 8x8 carpeted space along one of 24 long wide aisles.

Twenty-thousand officials and vendors walked past since it was a great place to hobnob. Pens and notebooks and carryall bags were the best attractors—everyone wanted one. But I didn't have those. I had color flyers on the table and free Life Savers candies. **Pathetic.**

A dozen business cards were left when the day was done, but I received no takers from follow-up calls and emails.

No wonder. **I had not presented who I was or the benefits of what I could offer well, not well at all. I had myself to blame. Benefits, not claims, always always sell better.**

Everyone is a stranger at first. Have a hook to attract them, solid offerings, and a hook to close the deal.

Think of a book. It has a genre that attracts specific readers. The first hook is the cover. Every chapter starts with a "hook;" an exciting action sequence, interesting characters, and story lines that keep readers engaged to the end of the chapter. Then a cliffhanger to get them to turn the page.

Good marketing and advertising uses hooks. If part of an exhibition, trade fair, or big venue where thousands pass by, consider hiring a display company to make/build an attractive display. Plan to use it again.

Frank got some solid leads.

Make sales by walking around

G

We achieved a huge positive result for our center at another indoor venue. We heard of an opportunity at the Richmond YMCA to set up our table. We also heard rumors that most people "north of the [James] Rivah" would not venture south of it to do business. It was that homes there were associated with old wealth in the northern section, and they seldom slummed by crossing the river.

South of the river comprised either commercial centers or subdivisions. However, we thought we would test the theory and try to attract wealthier clients. Ilene and I set up in the YMCA gym with another fifty tables, and over several hours forty or fifty people came by. To pass the time, Ilene and I traded places at the table, and on one of my excursions around the gym, I stopped by a table behind which sat two nurses. They represented a hospital only ten miles from our center.

I struck up a conversation and learned that the hospital could use our tutoring service for students who needed to take the TEAS—a standardized test required for entry into their nursing program.

This taught us that occasions arise with unexpected benefits. Although not one student came to us from anyone having stopped by our table at the YMCA, but within three years we had prepared dozens of students for TEAS, and nearly all scored enough to be admitted into the hospital program. **A definite marketing selling point.**

Share successes and kudos in your marketing and advertising. Measurable successes bring credibility, build reputation, and increase sales.

R

When promoting my own books, I attend Author Fairs in libraries, outdoor town squares, or street fairs. I pay a few bucks for table space, maybe split it with another author, or show at libraries for free. I lug my books and small display and hope it's crowded with book buyers.

It's tempting to sit in my chair behind the table and read a book or chat with authors. **But I don't do that. I am there to engage with passersby, to chat, talk, and inspire.** I stand at my display or nearby the whole time, look attentive, and try to catch their eye or interest without being obnoxious or in their face. A simple greeting: "How are you?" or "Anything you're looking for?" or "I'm the author. Any questions?" is enough to open a conversation. I always sell more books.

> *Mingle wherever you are by whatever means you can, using every media type available. Biz cards are cheap. 'Mingle' via social media and chatrooms too.*

At one fair, a customer picked up my memoir. As we chatted, I showed him my other books. He bought two volumes of essays as well. We got to know each other's tastes and likes. I gave him my card and got his email address.

He paid via PayPal on the spot.

An owner and their business must prove to be loyal to us before we give them our loyalty.

I realized I was the face of my books; the books weren't the face of me. **"Things" don't sell themselves; people do. The right marketing and relationships assure it.**

As an entrepreneur, have confidence in yourself, your product, or your service. You are "on" just like Robert Preston in *The Music Man* whenever you are in public. **Be natural. Open your mouth. Be a human.**

Whatever you offer, be personable and friendly.
Use conversational tones, speech, and formats.
Be interested in your prospect. Listen.

Offers out of the blue

G

Near the end of our first year of business, a woman called who oversaw the *Mommy & Me* program at a county mall a half hour from our business. She asked, "Would you be interested in filling in for a sponsor who could not be present for a segment of our program, *Nat Geo Kids*?"

I had grown up reading selected articles from *National Geographic Magazine* and marveled at the photographs, thinking how wonderful it would be to travel to exotic places. So, the opportunity piqued my interests.

"Absolutely! What would you like from us?"

> *When someone calls, always ask, "How can we help you?" At least, find out more about them.*

Fortunately, *National Geographic* provided a simple curriculum, and the materials for the program were provided by the mall administration. I made a colorful display with foam core and posters promoting them—and us. Our stint at the mall became one Saturday every month.

Again, we learned how important territory is to people who set up tables at events. Although we thought we deserved priority positioning because of helping the mall administration carry on its program, such was not the case. In all the time we were at the mall, we never got the ideal spot—in front of the entrance doors.

Another day we set the display up in front of a Barnes and Noble bookstore, thinking hordes of parents would visit it; however, only a paltry number entered. Occasionally our position was moved to a less desirable out-of-the way one, and Ilene even spoke to the event organizer about the situation, but to no avail. Upon reflection, the placement wasn't that important overall.

We continued our commitment at the mall, even though after three months we knew that simply "getting our name out there" and "paying it forward" to help us get to the next level wasn't working. We faced the fact we were not obtaining any clients just from promoting our business alongside the *Nat Geo Kids* presentation. We grew tired of devoting the time needed for preparation and delivery.

After our year's commitment, we no longer volunteered.

Volunteer

G

Unfortunately, our presence at other events did not bring us any clients either. These included volunteering at a state-wide Special Olympics event at the University of Richmond.

We began our assigned duties and focused on how we might obtain clients. As the games progressed, we saw how excited the children and adults in the competitions were. It was contagious. A positive atmosphere pervaded the stadium, one suffused with encouragement.

By the end, we were pleased we attended and helped make the Special Olympics a success. It no longer mattered that no one later contacted us. We were thrilled we added some joy.

Outdoor venues

Chester says: ***People like to go out. Street fairs, ballgames, parades, parks, eateries, concerts, celebrations, cookouts, and get-togethers are opportunities to hobnob, enjoy, and meet others.***

Purpose. We want, long for, and will fight for freedom and purpose. Freedom to freely associate, choose what we want, and go where we want to, are natural desires. Barriers and borders need to come down and fair policies put in place to ensure freedom to follow our path and purpose.

G

We learned quickly that jockeying for a position at indoor or outdoor venues instantly activates the area of the brain obsessed with private space and territory.

A light rain was falling when we arrived at the subdivision's clubhouse, expecting to be inside, a kick-off spot for a charity running event. Immediately we were told, "Sorry, you cannot set up inside, it's reserved for children's games."

We were there to raise money for a local girl with cancer, sad. We had our small folding table and display materials. The next best thing was to claim a tight spot on the porch, which was only five feet wide from the outer wall of the building to the rail.

We arrived early and negotiated a cramped space near the entrance next to where event coordinators sold tickets. We also had to convince a Mary Kay seller who wanted the same spot that people would see us and continue around the porch, stopping by her place after we mentioned her products.

I sweetened the deal by ordering two men's bath products I didn't need—that's how we did things back in Jersey. Luckily, too, we could suspend our banner on the railing so people would see us. Sure enough, during the hours we manned our table, even though people could barely move squeeze past the ticket sellers, we had a dozen people speak to us.

We handed out business cards and hoped for the best.

A few months later, one parent from the area who had seen our sign in the window recalled having seen us at the running event but did not hire us to do any tutoring.

Gauge your time available with expected traffic at the venue. Concentrate on bigger crowds.
Sales equals success, and more leads.

We also engaged in a walk-run event to raise funds to help cure cystic fibrosis. We also attended soccer games of three different students and cajoled cheerleaders at a nearby high school to include our flyers in their programs. Psychologically, all these ventures did more to make us feel a part of the community than to bring in business.

Use what works for the conditions. Tents and canopies work for outside.
Be prepared for the weather.

Chapter 52 Referrals and affiliates

Chester says: ***Take opportunities to branch out from your primary line of work. Start with a minimum investment of time and money.***

G

One thing we learned early is that if we weren't bringing in enough revenue through our primary business, we had to consider venturing into new territory.

A few months into our business, a woman approached us who had set up a counseling service for parents and their children who needed help to decide where to go to college. Should a high school student select a college based on its size, cost, distance from home, reputation, and programs? Or combine these factors?

We agreed to refer high school students to her for her advice, and she'd refer them to us for SAT/ACT preparation or for specific help. We had little success in this arrangement for several weeks, so I investigated becoming a certified college counselor myself. One organization that looked promising for me was the Higher Education Consultants Association (HECA).

It was hosting a conference in New Jersey, where my daughter lived. I rode a train to Trenton, where my daughter picked me up, and borrowed her car for a day.

I returned to Virginia with better knowledge of what a college counselor does and the responsibility of contacting college personnel in my geographical area; however, I it would mean too much time away from our fledgling business. It was like BNI became later, referral-based with potential, but iffy.

That process relied on the right circumstances, the right opportunity, and the right referral.

.

In 2023 Affiliate Marketing makes you recurring income from mentions and referrals.

Affiliate marketing and revenue

Affiliate marketing is a marketing arrangement in which affiliates receive a commission for each visit, signup, or sale made from their website, emails, or elsewhere that they generate for a merchant. This allows businesses to outsource and expand their sales and save costs.

Say I have an arrangement with Company X, who is a service or product seller (not a chief competitor). I talk about them, highlight them in my email listserv, or put their sales link on my website. If a viewer or customer on one of my social media, email, website, or ad outlets clicks Company X's link, that's a referral and I receive a commission from them that we've agreed on. If my link to them results in a sale for them, that amount to me should be bigger.

This is recurring revenue where I do very little. The best kind there is. It is a partnership. We share like interests.

How to find affiliates:
1. Reach out to similar vendors and niche bloggers
2. Look for key personalities, on social media too
3. Partner with industry influencers and experts
4. Search similar groups and forums
5. Invite existing customers

However, it's not always easy finding a company willing to agree to hookup without additional promotion on your part, since this method is now over-saturated. There are affiliate recruitment companies, but they charge. Fiverr.com is one.

Matt at mattmcwilliams.com offers 15 ways to find good matches by company, product, and even find an email address to write to. Check your industry for yours. **It's ideal to receive revenue from referrals. Don't we wish we could all do that?**

Note: If you send out an affiliate's sales link, it's fair to have a disclaimer, like "You should assume that the sender of this e-mail has an affiliate relationship to the providers of goods and services mentioned in this message and may be compensated when you purchase from them."

Don't get hemmed in

R I started ABLiA Media in 2012 to publish my own books. Then, through referrals and contacts, other writers came to me to edit theirs, so I became an editor. Then they asked for help publishing. I added that.

My website Services Page with pricing became more refined, with more offerings, attracting more writers. I added different rates for doing different edits, like books vs. short stories, even poetry anthologies. I was making more revenue in different ways and loving it, using my core talents and skills.

Don't get boxed in. Expand your thinking and offerings. Once you have mastered how to do one, add another.

The same applies to marketing and advertising. Don't get stuck on only one platform unless it produces significant results. There are new mountains on every horizon. You may want to hike one. Think outside the box.

If you plan well and produce good marketing materials for online, try a simultaneous campaign, even if small. This takes extra cash and time commitments, but gets your offerings more widely seen. **But to repeat, watch the Analytics and sales figures, and CTR conversions. Pull the plug if not producing profitable results.** Don't get sucked into "the sunk cost fallacy."

Chapter 53 Branch out and In

C*hester says: **Corporations buy up competitor companies every day. You can't do that yet, but you can steal good ideas and add business divisions whenever you want.***

G Ilene's venture into sewing was productive and brought in income. She began by teaching sewing, knitting, quilting, or crocheting to students we had tutored a while or who had shown an interest in such arts because of her conversations with their parents.

Since our learning center had an area in the rear with two five-foot tables, she set up her sewing machine there. Occasionally, she showed students the fundamentals of knitting. Students caught on, so Ilene offered project lessons. In one class of several students, a young boy was the first to finish a quilt. Ilene offered a variety, from simple placemats to dresses.

It was successful, and she established a subsidiary business: **Purse Garden**. Purse Garden became a home business of sewing either stuffed bears or bunnies out of the clothes of family members—usually deceased—or constructing and sewing quilts. She partnered with Valerie, a young woman who also helped with tutoring children.

The other business offshoot of our corporation became a program of offering paint parties, **Y'all Paint**. Originally, we permitted a woman with her own business of hosting paint parties to use our all-purpose room. However, she misinformed Ilene that the company that supplied picture templates had an exclusive agreement with her to do so. But such was not the case.

Ilene loved learning to paint from the woman and had mixed feelings about their separation, but she realized she could do paint parties herself. The process involved tracing images from a template onto a canvas using carbon paper, then creating an original painting.

Ilene pondered what to name her little business, and I was pleased to help. We were living in the South, so I came up with "Y'all Paint."

I helped her design a business card, and within a couple of years, with a Facebook page and word-of-mouth, Ilene averaged twenty people a month. We made little income from it, but a few parents signed up for costlier tutoring services.

Everything you do is woven together. Corporations have advantages in that they can have disparate side businesses under their umbrella.

R

Sole-proprietorships and LLCs have less autonomy in that they can't start new companies or subsidiaries the way corporations can, but they can branch out into related areas, even Divisions.

In 2012-2013, I published my first book, becoming an author. I started ABLiA Media to do so, which meant I was a company with advantages. It didn't take long as a critiquer of other writers' stories to expand to editing, which multiplied my income many times, and still does.

I put up my website, started a blog, and a weekly critique class at my library. I sent out emailed writing, publishing, and marketing tips weekly. I wrote more books and published 270 articles on an independent online blog. I joined poetry critique groups, attended workshops, and met hundreds of writers and poets. I was in touch with dozens of Baha'i friends and posted things on Instagram and Facebook and interacted there.

These contacts and interactions built up a large "tribe." Now 90% of my editing business is from repeat clients or their referrals. I can manage the work and am happy. A little advertising and marketing gave the cream taste to my cream soda for my income streams.

Issuing an emailed newsletter regularly to connect with contacts and customers is wise, and AI tools help compose, schedule, and keep track of everything. It's a wise marketing tactic.

Collect email addresses. If you send automated anything like a newsletter etc., have a Manage preferences or Unsubscribe link, and ask why they like or unlike it.

I also run contests or short giveaways with a top prize, a well-known book, or my eBooks, and run surveys, posted on social media, all to stay in touch and put a face to my typed voice.

With all of this, sales and recurring revenue increased.

Current contacts help you grow. Don't oversaturate them. It's not mass advertising; it's steady growth.

The secret of success equals a combination of Balance, Time, Planning, Preparation, Execution, and Follow-up.
The mighty 80-ft oak does not grow from its seed overnight.
Patience and persistence are part and parcel of successful enterprises, as well as flexibility and wisdom. **If you hold strictly to preconceived notions then your rigid business will topple over in a storm. Trees bend in strong winds.**

Expand

Chester says: *Some successful ventures may require little investment or time compared to others that need a lot but flop. Test, evaluate, learn, and hone.*

A physical store expands by increasing its footprint or floorspace, even moving to do so. Online stores, whether for products or services, expand and grow market presence with saturation. That means trying new target audiences, hoping to catch on, and repetition. You should start with a good guess and verify with Analytics. First, research or survey any market or customer profile you want to appeal to, then try it.

If you are not visible, you will remain invisible.
The Invisible Man didn't make out so well.

G

After a year of center operation and use of an online reading program, we realized more than a third of our tutoring students came to us for help in reading. Ilene was occasionally working as a substitute dental hygienist, and on one occasion struck up a conversation with a woman who was a reading specialist. Shelley had earned her doctorate in a midwestern university but was only applying her expertise as a volunteer in a local school's library once a week.

Ilene and I agreed that Shelley could become a valuable asset to our business. We offered her a job, and she jumped at it.

Hiring can be warm – with personal knowledge of the potential employee, or cold – from an application. Interviews are important.

Soon after she joined us, we thought we could expand by forming a subsidiary company, which we named Chesterfield Reading Clinic. No other reading clinics were in the county, and with Shelley handling young children and my handling older children, we met the needs of families and increased revenues.

Look for niches that fit your existing knowledge base, resources, and skills.

At the Center, we offered a low-cost alternative to expensive reading programs, including personal tutoring. The top four reading programs in the country required forkfuls of money to use their canned software, printed materials, and formats, ours didn't, and it was well-liked. **So, Ilene and I setup a new website just for reading,** and I cajoled Shelley into starring in a video based on an analogy I developed.

As Shelley was filmed, she spoke of imagining someone trying to catch a moving train. The more time that passed as one tried to get on board, the more difficult it would be. So too with reading.

On our website, we listed popular reading programs and truthfully stated that we drew from all of them to customize a reading program for each student. We produced some rack cards and business cards to promote our reading clinic.

Shelley went beyond our expectations. She offered small prizes for children who read a given number of books and created certificates for students that she and I signed.

Furthermore, Ilene created embroidered T-shirts that said, *I read 100 books at the Chesterfield Learning Center.*

Make your services special or have special touches unique to you. It's how you gain and retain customers and clients.

When we eventually downsized, Shelley set up a room in her home to tutor students, beginning with those who had been going to her for several months. This took away some of our students, but I was pleased she was successful.

Treat staff well and they will be loyal and hard-working. Use company revenue to determine bonuses and salary increases. Promote when deserved.

Salary increases include you too as the owner. Be fair. Longevity and quality of service should take someone far. Employees today change jobs, professions, and locations many times. Pay well to retain good ones or constantly grapple with high employee turnover and scheduling headaches.

R

If or when you need to hire, layout tasks beforehand that need to be done and how long they will take. It's best to create a Job Standards sheet and define what constitutes successful or non-successful completed tasks. This is critical when doing quarterly or annual employee performance evaluations. Good ratings result in a raise or bonus.

Hiring means scheduling and managing. Part-time staffing takes more coordination than full-time. In either, have a backup plan if an employee calls out sick. **High turnover is a sign of poor management, low salary, and little in benefits.**

Always have a three-month probation period for new staff, that's fair. Let them go if issues arise; it's your one chance to do it cleanly. I learned that lesson and let go a non-performing new hire before they came under Civil Service's further rules. Government is like that.

In private business, employees are hired "at will," and can be let go at will. But have a solid reason so you can avoid grievances or discrimination lawsuits.

A solid reason can be a poor economy, poor company income, a change in operations, or poor performance against standards.

The best bosses move around and don't stay sitting down. They don't micromanage. They guide and monitor but let staff use their own creativity and skills.

G

Another area we developed had limited success. Attempting to build on our connection with home-schooled children, I developed Branderwood Academy. The name was a blend of the two large development areas in which we were doing business: Brandermill and Woodlake.

The concept of an academy was derived from my research into what the term *academy* legally meant, and the extent to which we could draw families who didn't want to spend several thousand dollars for full-time enrollment in a private school. In Virginia, few restrictions apply to establishing an academy.

I thought the process would involve forming a board of trustees and getting the state to approve a charter, but all I had to do was come up with a name and advertise!

I spent hours developing courses of studies guided by a vision and a mission statement. I developed a program that accounted for forty-five hours of instruction per course, typical of a three-credit college course. I made booklets and advertised a meeting for anyone who might have an interest in such an academy.

Several home-schooling mothers showed up for the evening meeting, and while they understood the nature of the courses, none of them were prepared to spend the money to enroll their children. I deduced that no middle ground probably existed for parents unsatisfied with a public-school education: either they had the funds for a private school or didn't.

I learned over the years that many parents of underperforming home-school children would rather pay for dance, martial arts, or music lessons than for tutoring.

Before creating new programs or offering new services, do a "T" chart of pros and cons. Test it first.

Every plan or program, product, or service you offer and sell requires time, yours, or someone else's. Time is your most limited resource. <u>Don't burn yourself out.</u> **Money spent on the right help for the right task, for the right period of time, is $$$ and time well spent.**

Clocks and calendars are your friends, not enemies. Use them, abide by them, be prompt, and always on time.

YOU ARE YOUR BUSINESS.
You wear many hats, play many roles, and are chief cook and pots & pans washer. There's no supper without you.

Surveys grow your business

Chester says: **Surveys gather name and email address. Great for expanding market share and contacts. And knowing what you're doing right—or wrong.**

Printed on every receipt you receive from gas stations, drive-thru's, restaurants, and stores of every kind, is a code, a dotcom URL, a number to text, or QR code, asking you to take a survey. Do it and receive a prize, discount, gift, or link to join a Rewards Program. Why? **Companies vie for either or both your name and your email address to use in future marketing.**

They use survey answers to pinpoint demographics, and they love to know how much $$ you make. They love it when someone gives them top ratings, reviews, or testimonials.

SurveyMonkey, JotForms, Google Forms, QuestionPro, LimeSurvey, CrowdSignal, and ZohoSurvey are a few survey-making products. SurveyMonkey is one of the earliest and largest, has a free limited version, then goes up to over $1,400/mo and has Enterprise too. Each level has more features, bells & whistles, can hit more users, etc.

Start with a free one like Google Forms. Play with it. A short email survey is a great way to follow up a sale, test the market, or gauge market/brand awareness. Or generate awareness or interest. Surveys grow your contact email list. **They tell you who your customers are and what they like or don't. That's gold.**

Creating surveys is easy. Look for free templates and samples by category. Surveys can be timed to last a few hours, days, or be one-offs. Versatile.

For example, take Amazon for product purchases and Microsoft for their online Get Help staff engagements. They and just about all other companies' survey buyers and users after an interaction. My Honda dealer does too after every repair or car purchase.

Examine how they do it and what they ask. Keep it short and simple, 5 questions. Smart companies take responses seriously and gage employee performance and product benefits or faults. You will too. They can offer something else you're selling too.

Properly conducted surveys gather data, lead to positive reviews, and can sell. Every business or product or service needs positive reviews. Gather results or percentages, emails, or testimonials and use them in promotions.

R

Annual summaries/percentages of positive vs. negative survey results on every company out there should be mandatory for every mid-sized and large business in America. It wouldn't be daunting like the annual Consumer Reports Annual Car Survey, but I'd love to see ratings for Company Reliability and Customer Support at least.

Speaking of Consumer Reports, bless them.

Critical unbiased or grassroots reports are a boon. **Magazines, blogs et al. run Top 10 or 20 product comparisons all the time on every item or service imaginable. Refer to them liberally.**

In your Surveys:
- **Collect names**
- **Collect emails**
- **Evaluate company a/o employee performance**
- **Find what works well**
- **Discover what is liked or hated**
- **Gain positive reviews**
- **Ask, "Would you be interested in…?" (upsell)**

Experience and knowledge go far to expand sales. Be an information gatherer. Google, Facebook, Amazon, Microsoft, and others are masters of that.

Partnering

Partnership marketing is a collaborative arrangement with another business that's mutually beneficial. It helps both reach new customers and/or build new relationships. Watch ads closely. Don't be surprised to see multiple brands shown.

G

Our best success was partnering with a day-care center that transported children to our learning center to enjoy a Lego camp. The goal was for the participants to plan a community made of Legos and then build it. The elementary-aged students cooperated well, and Ilene and I could run the program without hiring another tutor to help.

We also learned that while a particular program might be successful one year, it may not be the next. For example, a summer camp program on scrapbooking, while successful in the early years of business, ceased to appeal to students because of the popularity of online programs such as Shutterfly.

We announced an Easter party at our first learning center, and a few dozen families joined us, and a few other businesses sponsored games and activities. Families came, and we had a good time, but not one family signed up his or her child for tutoring lessons. The result is that we discovered that for our learning center, Facebook posts were most successful in informing people of educational ideas, not offering deals.

Radio, tv, and internet access is 24/7. These services and applications only get more popular and ubiquitous as time passes. Government is switching everything to online.

Movie ticket anyone?

Another idea Ilene and I had was to ask a movie theater to allow us to provide a free movie ticket to anyone who signed up for a tutoring lesson. We spent a weekend sitting behind our table with its banner in front of a movie theater but had no takers.

How things have changed! Years ago, sales were face-to-face, now it's phone, text, or email, some onscreen.

R

Professional salespeople are trained hard and often by their companies. Being personable, overcoming objections, touting benefits, negotiating terms or price all add up to conversions and sales. **But hard, pushy sales techniques rarely sit well.**

Face-to-face seals deals. Word of mouth. To be at your best-selling game, take some sales courses. Learn how to be charming yet firm. One minute no nonsense, flexible the next, cajoling the next. And know when to be which.

Mostly it's human personable techniques, phrases, rhetorical questions, and logic that overcome "No," and get to "Yes."

Human and honest qualities go far when speaking with people. One is: Get to the point! Everyone's time is valuable, so don't bend their ear all day. **Good products and services sell themselves on their own merits. Don't defend.**

Retail sales means "The price is the price." "Negotiated" means let's talk. Wholesale is distribution before retail sales & for large quantities.

Few can negotiate well with a faceless, voiceless person or company that sits unseen behind a computer screen. You must learn to. For in-home or in-store sales, that's who you are, and that's what you must do. It's important you have the facts about your target audience, their wants, and needs, and show you have what will service them.

233

Chapter 54 Aftershock

C hester says: ***Pay bills when due, or account, credit rating, cash flow, or legal problems may ensue.***

We all need things. Like dough. For buying and paying for goods and services, which are now available anywhere in hundreds of choices. In commerce, the days of bartering services or goods as a common occurrence are rare. **Buying brings one obligation: pay now or later.**

Even "free" items come with fine print or a limited time.

G

Eight months after having left our old learning center location for the new and improved one, we received a letter from a law firm representing our former leasing company.

It was not a "return receipt requested" or anything similar.

At this point in our business, we had finally reached what I had set as a goal before we took in any money for ourselves: a company bank balance of $25,000. It was as though this number jinxed us. This letter said we owed $9,000 in penalties to our former landlord because a few rent payments over a three-year period had been a few days late. We thought about ignoring it, but since we were dedicated to keeping honest dealings in all transactions, I called our old leasing company.

We had been told the day of our vacancy that everything was fine, but this was done orally on site. This made no difference to the company now because it was losing so much money on the entire shopping center, of which we had been a minor part. We were not the only business to have vacated.

We surmised other landlords were losing $160,000 per month compared to a few years ago. No wonder they came after us!

A summons directed us to report to a court in Norfolk, two hours away, which confirmed we disputed the claim. Following that would be an assigned day during which we would have to present evidence in our favor.

We contacted a lawyer and were reminded how attorneys make five times what I did per hour. We informed the attorney that we did not want to spend more than $800, but his last bill was $1,000.

---
*Hire professionals when needed.
It's an investment. Get details in writing.*

However, the money was well spent. With their help, we ended up paying $4,500 not $9,000, half what the leasing company demanded. A few months later, the leasing company filed for bankruptcy, and a bank took over the strip mall. From this point on, Ilene and I resolved all bills had to be paid before they were due. We could not afford a costly repetition.

We also learned that all checks written to our business had to be cashed in or deposited before closing our business account: this was a matter we overlooked, so we were out a few hundred dollars. Ilene and I had, from the first opening, also agreed we would pay all credit card balances when due. This prevented paying high interest on monthly payments. We also never took Cash Advances, which accrued extra high interest immediately.

Use credit wisely. Pay off balances quickly. Avoid Cash Advances. **Interest payments are lost profits.**

The total experience showed us again how important it was to check contract terms, make notes, and plan accordingly. Setting due dates was important also.

Chapter 55 Downsizing

Chester says: ***Easing out of a business may be more frustrating than rewarding. When forming a business, plan to dissolve it.***

Decide the income you need

You have multiple sources of income. Personally, it may be a part time job, severance pay, retirement checks, Social Security, savings etc. Income comes from your company services or product sales, loans, and other things you sell, like options or one-offs.

But from all income, two categories of expenses fit in one big bucket. Fixed costs are set (even though some vary monthly) like rent, utilities, taxes, insurance, loan repayments, and monthly or annual fixed software license costs.

Discretionary costs can be cut, like advertising, training, maintenance, vacations, and travel (automobiles), even tobacco or liquor, and entertainment. If you can cut down usage or go without for a time, it's discretionary, i.e. avoidable, like some supplies, mailing, etc.

As owner/operator, you must have a salary too!

Not later, but sooner. Like we said in Chapter 1, you may be supporting only yourself, or your family, too. Maybe this is a sideline gig until it really takes off. **Whatever it is, you deserve a share of the income!**

Depending where you reside it may be plus or minus expensive to live. 2023 apartment rents go from $1,200 to $1,800/mo plus. Houses cost more regardless of interest rates, and it's a buyer's market—they sell in a few days in bidding wars. Food is more expensive, even coffee at Wawa, Panera, or Dunkin. Restaurant prices have increased dramatically, even the price of eggs at $7.00/dozen, and the usual staples in grocery stores. Bakery goods and meat have skyrocketed.

The East and West coasts are more expensive, the South and Midwest, less. How are you coping with that? **Make your business pay you fairly. It's a business expense like others. Don't be foolish and put it off.** Start doing it when you are in the black, even if small.

If at some point the business can't pay you a decent salary, after trying all you can to make it work, sit down at your kitchen table. Take out your business plans, marketing plan, goals, objectives, and ledger sheets. Review, readjust, rethink, regroup. Look at all agreements, expenses, ad campaigns, income successes, and failures. Make a T-Chart. It's time to make changes and continue, or to dissolve and go a different route. **Be smart.**

Do not beat a dead horse with your personal money. Remember, you can start almost any small business you want to. You may not be forced to stop being your own boss. That's why rainy-day funds are in every business budget.

Whether young, in between, or old

C hester says: ***The world of Commerce welcomes solopreneurs and entrepreneurs. Every age has benefits. Retirement can be rewarding.***

G

At my 50th high school reunion in August 2016, I learned I was the only person not retired. The following March, my father-in-law, with whom I was extremely close, passed away.

Both factors convinced me I should retire as soon as our center's lease ran out at the end of June. However, a few parents contracted with me to continue tutoring in the summer, and my intention was to tutor in a local library.

Also, Ilene was less enthusiastic about closing, and when a friend of hers informed her of a place that had a small office for rent, she arranged to visit it. Not only was the cost only $600 per month, but utilities were included, and it overlooked a scenic reservoir.

Japan has businesses dating from 578 CE. Companies can last long when managed well and operated with foresight, planning, and good management. Some establishments in Europe are hundreds of years old.

Ilene excitedly told me about the place, and when I saw it, I admitted it had the possibility of greater profit for less effort than did our last two locations. I had envisioned our tutoring a maximum of fifteen students and referring any number beyond that to the tutors whom we had employed for the last few years.

Although the office seemed adequate for our needs, I was reluctant to rent it, for we would be subleasing from a non-mainstream religious organization. Nevertheless, our contact, Michael, seemed genuine in his desire to have us as a tenant. He agreed to give us the last two weeks in June to set up before we had to pay monthly rent.

We had everything we needed in terms of supplies, equipment, and materials from the current office, but we realized we might need to tutor more than one student at a time in the small office, about 80 square feet—compared to 2500 square feet of the other office. We purchased a table online, rearranged the desk, filing cabinet and bookcase donated from the previous renter, and set up the optimum configuration.

And we had enough students—including those who wanted mathematics instruction—to rent a second room on Tuesdays and Thursdays. We continued the employment of our most veteran mathematics tutor. Within a couple of weeks, we realized we would like the use of that second office space on a full-time basis, so arranged to rent it full time and altered the lease accordingly.

Several students wanted instruction in both English and mathematics for standardized tests, and so we had a core income stream.

Most important goals: 1. Establish core income sources. 2. Have the customers 3. Don't spend more than you have. 4. Pay yourself and others a fair salary.

Feeling I could be more selective as to the students I would tutor, I altered our fee structure for the first time in several years. I was frankly tired of students' parents signing up for tutoring a lesson when only convenient for them; this complicated our scheduling and gave them more opportunity to cancel a lesson.

The new fee schedule insisted on parents signing up for six, twelve, eighteen, or twenty-four lessons, and I raised the prices slightly. To my pleasant surprise, no parents objected.

By the middle of July, we had twenty students signed up, and could keep our math tutor as busy as she liked while raising her pay from $25 to $35 per hour.

*Retain key employees by paying them well.
Avoid high employee turnover.*

The tutor agreed to pay half the cost of the new room, but in the accounting, including added expenses of using a credit card machine, resulted in our receiving only a few dollars' profit per student. Since she was supporting both herself and her husband, within a month, we stopped charging her rent, reducing our income significantly.

We believed the rooms in which we tutored could easily be viewed as confining and not as professional as parents might think for tutoring their children. Therefore, I made it a point to discuss tutoring in a professional-looking conference room upstairs.

While the building and its view of the lake were impressive, our rooms were not, and I found that our percentage of potential clients signing up for our services dropped dramatically from those associated with our former place.

Looking back at our decision to continue the business, I regret it.

We discovered our goal for 2017 was to make just enough money to allow each of Ilene and me able to reach the maximum amount allowable under social security limits to prevent us from having to suffer a penalty.

We barely made that limit.

We closed for good and dissolved the Chesterfield Learning Center having given it our best efforts. But time and age changed our circumstances and energy to go on. I tutored two students at our own home for a few months after moving out from our third tutoring location.

I'm still privately tutoring today.

Goals change. Don't be afraid of change.

Learning Center reflections

C hester says: ***Running a small business is not just about acquiring wealth and prestige. It's being of service.***

G

It took a few months to understand the monetary aspects of running and growing a business. From the get-go, the main recurring expense was the Learning Center's lease or rent, followed by utilities, paying our "flexible" salaries, and paying the tutors. Incidentals included supplies, gas for our two cars, advertising, and the cost of computers and internet access. Along the way, we had tried many promotion and advertising ideas that had not generated meaningful business.

As I discovered, most lessors provide a lessee with a few months' free as an incentive to signing on for a three-year contract. After we had found what we believed to be an appropriate place for our business, we signed a contract, but we did not understand the finer points of the lease.

One thing we learned was that a contract for three years included a stipulation that if we did not want to renew, we had to provide notice to the company six months before it ended.

Go through legal documents and draw up a calendar of To Do's.

We also learned that every year the leasing company could raise the monthly rent rate for things like snowplowing. Our rate increased from $2,350 per month to $2,554 after one snowstorm.

Unforeseen obligated expenses like that hurt us.

We did not make advertising a line-item in our budget. A big mistake. We simply responded to opportunities when the time arose. **We should have set up a monthly budget and let the money accumulate until a new opportunity and mode of advertising arose.**

Having been a teacher for nineteen years, I knew how much the job entailed. I paid our tutors a good salary starting at $20 an hour. One tutor who traveled forty minutes to our center got paid $25 for the first hour of tutoring. When we hired a chemistry tutor who had a PhD, we paid $25 per hour.

We closely monitored our weekly income by using a Google calendar. Above each day's listing, we would place the amount of money we had received that day. In our first few months of operation, it was about $500 per month—not enough to meet expenses.

By our third year, we were earning enough to pay ourselves back from our home equity line of credit. By our fifth year, Ilene and I could earn regular salaries. It was well within the limit imposed by the Social Security Administration for not having to face a penalty for excess income.

When we moved to our second location, we paid less money per month than we had at the first place. At the height of our business, we were taking in a few thousand dollars a week from 70 hours' tutoring time.

To save money over time, we purchased a laser printer and contracted for air conditioning and heating maintenance. We also purchased our ink jet cartridges when on sale because we used four other printers/copiers along with computers. We dropped our fax line when we moved to our second location, and we made our own sandwiches and salads for lunch.

However, in our third location, we barely kept up with expenses—especially since we paid our best tutor $35 per hour. It was our way of helping her as we eased out of the business.

And ease out, sadly, we did. But in 2023, I still tutor. And write books. And live, have fun, and enjoy it. And Ilene and I are together.

LLC reflections

R

When I realized after three years of trying to get RREnergy off the ground that it had failed, I knew I hadn't gotten my name out enough or attracted the right clients to my energy skill set.

After doing a list of pros and cons, it was a simple decision. I wasn't making money. I discovered I loved writing. Writing my memoir was great fun. Why not help others publish and earn $$? Editing was the next step on that path. So, I pivoted. A free WIX website and ABLiA Media was born.

I told my writing classes and writer friends what I was doing, and immediately a few signed up. It was a sign.

I haven't looked back. I'm happy. My clients are happy, and I make $$. Opportunities are everywhere.

Don't be afraid to pivot.

Epilogue to Volume 2

In the Introduction we said it could be overwhelming. We've covered many bases and emphasized marketing and advertising because word needs to get out, especially online.

But you already know more than you ever thought possible. You're human and have experienced life. Like all of us, you are a buyer and seller. You've grown up in the huge marketplace of products and services, prices and discounts, marketing and advertising, and seeing or hearing 4,000 to 10,000 ads or commercials per DAY.

Just keep to your passion and your purpose. Keep taking one step after the other. Ada Lovelace did it. Mao did it. Nelson

Mandela did it. Barack Obama did it. Rosa Parks did it. George Washington did it. Marie Curie did it. Anna Bissell did it. Jeff Bezos and Bill Gates did it. You will to.

Making business work—George & Ilene

Starting and running our businesses was rewarding.

As our business grew, we hired additional tutors, two of whom depended on Chesterfield Learning Center salaries to make ends meet. They taught math, reading, art, and general science. Initially offering tutoring for French, we expanded into areas of Spanish, German, and Chinese.

We were challenged by requests to hire science tutors for chemistry and physics, but our diligence paid off.

Making connections was essential for keeping the business viable. After a year, not only had we established good rapports with district principals and school counselors, but also with the superintendent. **By our second year, word-of-mouth brought in more business, and some parents used us for years.**

We learned from our mistakes and relied on level-headed Chester to advise us. It's important to find out from other businesspeople what recommendations they have for specific services, and how, when, and where to advertise.

In our own case, we found that buying expensive billboards was not worth the money, nor were full-page ads in school yearbooks. Advertising on shopping carts or buying business-card-sized ads on menus, church bulletins, or local papers brought in only a few students.

We knew because we always asked how they heard of us.

After leaving Virginia and settling in New Jersey, Ilene and I benefited from past experience. As I began tutoring one-to-one with students in person or through Zoom, I used the skills I learned when operating the Chesterfield Learning Center with Ilene. Keeping accurate financial records, updating my Google calendar every week, and maintaining frequent communication with parents of students became second nature.

In retrospect, we are proud we helped hundreds of students increase their knowledge, grow to love reading, improve their grades, and be accepted into the colleges of their choice. Some of our tutors became like family, and we enjoyed interacting with them and knowing we provided them with income.

Running a business, while it has challenges and disappointments, taught us valuable lessons on how to interact with people. It provided us with a deep sense of accomplishment, too.

We trust you will benefit from our experiences and tips while you interact with others and bring in income to make your life more pleasurable and rewarding. **It makes an enormous difference if you can maintain joy for what you do.**

Best wishes to everyone willing to try.

Life and joy can come together—Rod

We most often think of passion as romance—a passionate embrace or kiss, a flirtation or roll in the sack. Passion seems strongest in our youth, and it takes effort and understanding of what it truly is to maintain or redirect it.

After Catholic schooling, public school exploded my mind in 1964. I was a good learner although slow to apply learning. My first jobs at 15 were selling magazines door to door and tarring roofs. I broke into a department store. I was in trouble a lot.

So, I was packed off to a three-year stint with my bachelor Dad in California to keep me out of jail again, first delivering home newspapers then cleaning office buildings. I got my driver's license at 16, back to Jersey and met my high school sweetheart, and back West again to a free junior college.

Unfulfilled and lost without my energetic red-headed girlfriend, I bussed back to Jersey to feed geriatric patients in the Trenton State Psychiatric Hospital, then transferred to a stock clerk job for the Bureau of Data Processing when 20. After 9 years of operating IBM mainframes, I began a professional career dealing with Information Technology contracts, added Energy in 2003, and retired in a buy-out.

I had passions for learning, reading, and writing, and the love of my life, Janet. I continued those loves into my first home business, RR Energy, and pivoted into ABLiA Media for writing, editing, and publishing.

> **Who cares? What's my message?**

People and writing gave me passion. It guides me, but it took years to draw it out. With two volumes on business, 2 memoirs, 270 essays in books and online, 2 poetry anthologies, and helping writers, I am immersed in what I love.

Passion gave me a new reality. To be something, someone, if not to others at least to myself and Janet, our kids and theirs, to relatives and friends, my coworkers also. In that reality I don't use alcohol anymore to guffaw and have "a good time," or to exploit sexual dalliances anymore, or to be a fanatic Phillies and Eagles fan, although I cheer them on.

In my new reality, religion included, I became more interested in life, in others, what was going on locally, and in the world at large. I cared.

Find and feed your loves. Don't let time, doubts, or naysayers thwart you. Resources, even cash, are out there. Use expert knowledge and wisdom readily available. You know more than you think. If it's exciting, challenging, legal and ethical, go for it. **With a little money, smarts, a good name, a decent reputation, and your best efforts, it'll pay off.**

Be lovable. Love yourself. Be yourself and make others happy. Trust in a higher power. Reflect on yesterday, act today, and plan for tomorrow.

> **Don't dream of being your own boss.**
> **Be one. Stay one. A good one.**

Caio and good fortune, Rod

Appendix A Sample

Editing Services Agreement
between
_____(Name of company)___ (herein "The Company"),
a __(State of ____)__registered for-profit business, and
___(Name of client)__of _(town, State)_ (herein "The Client")

Company will provide services required by Client as follows:

1.0 Company will edit and improve manuscript including:
1. Review all submitted manuscript pages or part thereof;
2. Suggest improvements and changes to improve the clarity, flow, story arc, tone and style;
3. Suggest improvements via MS-Word redline and Comments which can be consulted upon by phone;
4. Improve or correct vocabulary, tense, grammar, and syntax (copy editing);
5. Format the manuscript for greatest impact;
6. Identify missing details to improve the manuscript;
7. Identify better phrasing, sentence, and paragraph structures;
8. One hour of phone consultation for every 25 pages returned to Client. Additional time arranged by mutual agreement.
9. Up to 25 edited pages returned to Client within 3-5 days of receipt, delivered electronically to Client.
10. Email communications preferred and returned same or next day.

2.0 Fees: All fees quoted are firm throughout the Agreement. In consideration of services to be provided as described above, Client agrees to remit to Company the following amounts in U.S. dollars:
  A. Nonrefundable Advance Fee of __($)___received before editing begins.
  B. For 8.5x11 typed single-spaced or in MS-Word digital format: payment of __($)__per word reviewed, in three near-equal payments, at beginning, midway, and final;
  C. For 6x9 trade size typed single-spaced, __($)__ for additional formatting.

Company final charge based on total manuscript words reviewed and formatted for the publication size chosen less payments made. Client may request Expediting at an additional fee per page to be delivered sooner upon agreement with Company by email of delivery date and price.

3.0 Limitations on manuscript: Must be MS-Word 2019, 2016 or 2013 or compatible. Manuscripts up to 80,000 words accepted. Fees negotiated and agreed to in advance for longer lengths, unique sizes, or submissions in other formats. The Company does not offer ghostwriting service. Company reserves the right to refuse service for valid reason(s).

4.0 Cancellation. Either party may cancel in writing at anytime. Company will attempt to give Client at least 14 days' notice unless unavoidable circumstances arise. Outstanding fees are due and payable up until time of cancellation.

> **5.0 Default and Remedies.** If Company fails to deliver all pages to be reviewed by agreed upon delivery date(s) for any reason, Client's sole remedy will be return of the uncompleted manuscript, with charges due only for completed work. If Client fails to pay Company amounts due upon agreed upon terms, Company may file for breach and seek remedies.
>
> **6.0 Liability.** Company disclaims all responsibility for reliance by Client on Company's formats, edits, revisions, or proofing in whole and in part. Company comments, questions, statements of supposed fact, suggested changes or modifications are suggestions only. It is the Client's duty and sole responsibility to accept, modify, or reject the Company's reviews based on Client's own verifications and judgments. Client agrees to use Company's manuscript reviews at Client's own risk. Client agrees Company is absolved of all present and future liabilities.
>
> **7.0 Jurisdiction.** Client agrees to the laws of the State of ___(insert)___ regarding contract law, without regard to principles of conflict of laws, which will also include unresolved disputes.

_____("Company name")

SIGNED_____
(Title)_____
(Print name)_____
Date_____
Email _____Phone_____

_____("Client name")

SIGNED:_____
(Title)_____
(Print name)_____
Date: _____
Email_____Phone_____

Appendix B Sample Rack Cards

Other Resources

Free resources for small businesses are vast. Help is always out there.

- Amazon Small Business Academy https://www.smallbusiness.amazon/sign-up
- Brief, topical, emailed newsletters are great. Google what you need or want info on. Sign up for those in your industry.
- Improve financial literacy with https://www.fdic.gov/resources/consumers/money-smart/money-smart-for-small-business/index.html
- Find grants at https://www.grants.gov/. Grants may be based on your income for your last fiscal year.
- Setup and learn Quickbooks at https://www.score.org/santabarbara/event/setting-quickbooks-recorded-webinar Go on SCORE.org for many more.
- Rely on https://www.BusinessNewsDaily.com or Forbes.com
- SCORE.org is affiliated with the Small Business Administration (SBA). It also has volunteer experienced mentors you can meet with via Zoom or GoToMeeting, and personal help on your Business Plan, or a Marketing Template and hundreds of resources, **all free.**
- Scan books on "How to Sell" like Zig Zigler's *Secrets on Closing the Sale*, and Google "How to become successful in business." Check out *The Lean Startup* for entrepreneurs by Eric Ries.
- Keep tabs on competitors. Find info on how here https://www.michiganstateuniversityonline.com/resources/leadership/ways-to-better-understand-your-competitors/

About the Authors

George I. Martin EdD

A 160-acre abandoned farm in the Adirondack Mountains of New York gave George a home with a love of the outdoors and respect for nature. He attended a central school with only 23 students in his graduating class. George earned a bachelor's and a master's degree in education at Plattsburgh State University College.

After having taught English at a junior high school during the day and a maximum-security prison in the evenings, George and his first wife moved to Virginia, where he taught at a military prep school for fourteen years.

He was offered a full scholarship to attend the University of Virginia, where he obtained his Doctor of Education in English.

Over the next years, George taught education and English courses full-time at three universities and part time at several other colleges and universities. During that time, he published articles in professional journals and turned to creative writing.

After owning and operating Chesterfield Learning Center for seven years with his second wife Ilene, George retired to tutor students in English/ language arts while devoting time to writing. Some of his experiences were published this year in *Episodes at Intervals*, on Amazon.

You can reach George at writeagain2022@gmail.com

Rodney Richards

I roamed Trenton NJ streets as an untamed juvenile of the '50s and '60s. In 1970, my dark city soul about-faced and embraced the Baha'i Faith's spiritual and moral guidance. A year later, Janet, my red-headed high school sweetheart and I married.

We later settled into a suburban rancher, had our son, and I discovered I was bipolar. Once stable, we had our daughter and within 15 years were well-established career professionals, Janet as an elementary teacher and me in contract negotiations and bidding IT and energy for the state.

Retiring in 2009, I began writing prose & poetry. In 2012, I started a weekly library writing group that still meets. ABLiA Media began the same year. Besides my published books, essays, and poems, I taught technical and business writing to Princeton high schoolers for three years, and one year of nonfiction writing at Night School.

I strongly believe everyone should share their story.

Jan and I live in Central Jersey, are world citizens, and enjoy our entertaining grandchildren along with a blessed life.

Visit https://rodneyrichards.info for info on my company
Or check https://LinkedIn.com/in/rodneyrichards19
Say Hello at https://www.facebook.com/rodneywriter
See how I stay hopeful at https://www.bahai.org

If you can take a moment to leave a review wherever you purchased this from, George and I would appreciate it.
I would love to hear from you at 1950ablia@gmail.com

Call me Rod